Up With The Lark

Up With The Lark

My Life on the Land

JOAN BOMFORD

𝐇

HODDER &
STOUGHTON

First published in Great Britain in 2015 by Hodder & Stoughton
An Hachette UK company

1

Copyright © Joan Bomford 2015
With thanks to Matt Whyman

Images on page 196 and 200 © Christian Barnett.
All other images courtesy of the Bomford family.

A CIP catalogue record for this title is available from the British Library

Hardback ISBN 978 1 4736 2697 3
Ebook ISBN 978 1 4736 2700 0

Typeset in Bembo by Hewer Text UK Ltd, Edinburgh

Printed and bound by CPI Group (UK) Ltd, Croydon, CR0 4YY

Hodder & Stoughton policy is to use papers that are natural, renewable
and recyclable products and made from wood grown in sustainable forests.
The logging and manufacturing processes are expected to conform to
the environmental regulations of the country of origin.

Hodder & Stoughton Ltd
Carmelite House
50 Victoria Embankment
London EC4Y 0DZ

www.hodder.co.uk

I dedicate this book to my late husband, best friend and soul mate
'Tony'
Anthony Lawrence Bomford
1933–2014

And to my brother
John Collins
1936–2012

Contents

Prologue: A Scrap of a Girl   ix

PART ONE

1 The Journey Home   3
2 Gentle Giants   9
3 Brother John   15
4 Loyalty and Love   22
5 'Ain't Got a Boy at All   29
6 Lights Out   36
7 The War Ag   42
8 The Trusted   50
9 Home Guard   57
10 The Elephant that Came to Stay   65
11 Two Fronts   72

PART TWO

12 Man's Land   81
13 Young Farmers   87
14 Two is Company   94
15 Flight of Fancy   101
16 Irene   108
17 A Test of Motherhood   116

PART THREE

18	A Herd and a Home	125
19	About the Car	132
20	Trespassers	139
21	The Bomford Boys	146
22	Building a Dream	153
23	The Boom Years	160
24	Battles	167
25	Flood Water	174
26	The Steam Whistle	182
27	The One Landed Orchard	188
28	Up with the Lark	196
	Epilogue: My Horses, My Life	200
	Acknowledgements	211

PROLOGUE
A Scrap of a Girl

My sister Marian and I with Great Aunt Maud.

Fond memories await me as soon as I open the farmhouse door.

The squeak of the hinges is enough to take me back to when I grew up here. The stone tiles in the kitchen might be worn down through the ages, but it feels like only yesterday that I would watch my mother clean and polish them so thoroughly. It also reminds me of my dad; diligently unlacing his boots at the threshold so he didn't bring mud inside.

In the late afternoon light, shadows fall through the windows just as they did when I was a child. I only have to close my eyes to think of the life, love, drama and laughter that have occurred within these walls. But it's what lies beyond, out there in the fields, where my heart will always belong.

This is Quarry Pits Farm in the parish of Dormston, and the place where I grew up. The house is nestled at the foot of a short but steep slope. A two-storey red brick building with slate tiles and panelled windows, it's tucked away from the lane and commands a view across rolling pasture and pockets of woodland. Church towers punctuate the landscape in places, rising up from behind gentle folds that hide villages like nearby Inkberrow. On a clear day, far beyond to the west, the Malvern Hills take shape like a pencil trace on the horizon. It's the kind of place where you can watch clouds sail all the way across the sky and completely change shape along their course. The small quarry and brickyard, from which the farm acquired its name, is located a little further up the lane. Hidden behind hedgerow, the yard closed for business in the late 1800s. It effectively returned to a wilderness state, while the house and the acres surrounding it went on to thrive.

I will always feel at home on a farm like this one. It's in my bones, as it has been for generations of my family. And today I'm here to reflect upon my past so that I might share my story. I'm into my ninth decade, but like to think you wouldn't know it. My stride has shortened, but my recollections are as clear as a summer's day. I am fortunate in many ways, despite the challenges I've faced throughout my years as a farmer's daughter, a farmer's wife, and a farmer in my own right.

It's a life that brought me unexpected attention recently, and an award that leaves me lost for words. Gazing out from my old bedroom, at my beloved barn and the pasture land beyond, I think of that scrap of a girl with soil under her fingernails and wonder how on earth she grew up to be considered a 'Farming Hero'. So, this is where I begin, in a treasured farmhouse in the heart of Worcestershire ...

PART ONE

I

The Journey Home

Two of the steam engines my dad collected on the day I was born.

My father held on to witness my birth before setting out on the road. He didn't want to leave, as he stressed when telling me this tale. But work was a necessary way of life for my dad. Normally, it wouldn't take him further than the fields. But on that day in 1932 he had to travel far.

'I'll be as quick as I can,' he had assured my mother, and then looked sheepishly at the cap in his hands. They both knew speed would not be on his side.

'Could you wait a little while?' she asked, and cupped the back of my little head. 'Another day, perhaps?'

My dad began to turn his cap.

'I have to provide,' he said. 'If I miss the opportunity it won't just be this family that loses out.'

'Then promise me you'll take care,' she said from her bed, propped up on pillows and holding me close.

'It's you I worry about.'

Mother smiled reassuringly. I was no more than two hours old, a stranger to them all, but my mum was quite comfortable holding me. A maternal woman, she could still look calm and serene despite the labour she had been through.

'We're quite safe here,' she said as if to remind him.

Just then, a sense of peace had settled in place of the drama and expectation that accompanied my arrival. Sunlight streamed through the window, catching specks of dust, while the floorboards creaked like a ship at sea when Father shifted his weight from one foot to the other. He returned his attention to my mother, so striking and relaxed with her dark hair unpinned and the baby in her arms. She possessed a quiet beauty, and a calming presence that would form the core of our family life.

'Let's hope the weather holds,' said Father, as if unsure how to say goodbye.

Mother nodded. She understood just what he meant. My sister, just two at the time, stood at the bedside and stared at the new arrival. Grasping the edge of the blankets with both hands, she studied me closely as if seeking to work out what difference my presence might make to her life. My mum turned her attention to us both in turn. 'Come rain or shine, what matters most is that you make it home in one piece,' she told him. 'We're all depending on you.'

Like my sister and me, and the generation on each side of us, Colin John Halford Collins was born at Quarry Pits. With one hundred acres of pasture, stretched across hillside and lowland on both sides of the lane, the farm provided him with his livelihood. As a boy, following the death of his own father in an accident with a pony and trap, Colin Collins had helped his mother keep the place up and running. Keenly aware of his calling, he had grown up to take over completely. Ultimately, my dad was uncompromisingly hard working, with a commitment to the fields as a means of providing for his family. As well as tending to his cattle and crops, he contracted out agricultural machinery – including the crew to operate it – to farmers across the county and beyond. He rarely stopped, in fact, what with the maintenance and management, and I sometimes wonder if that's what took him to an early grave.

I was born into an age of steam. The era we all know in history books might've just come to an end, with the railways and the factories turning to diesel and electricity, but in the fields one source of power thrived. Ploughing engines were commonplace on agricultural land. These giant, immensely strong beasts were far more effective at hauling than a team of Shire horses, but much depended on the ground. On heavy clay soil, such as the fields at Quarry Pits and the surrounding farms, we had to rely on a different, more labour-intensive system. It involved the use of not one engine but two, and the prospect of acquiring a new pair is what took Father away from the family on the day that I was born.

Leaving the farmhouse behind, and the loved ones in his life, my dad headed up the sloped path to where his other pride and joy awaited him. There she stood, her chrome wire wheels and running boards gleaming in the sun, just waiting for his attention. When he started up the engine, that throaty roar made him feel good to be alive. The Morgan was an open-top roadster that boasted a blistering speed for the time as well as a unique appearance. For this model was fitted with a little back seat, despite sporting just one wheel at the rear, and looked as precarious as it was fun to drive. And so Father set about picking up passengers for a trip across the country that guaranteed every moment would be memorable.

Inkberrow and Stowmarket lie some one hundred and fifty miles apart. Driving at a lick, the Morgan got my dad to his destination within a few hours along with four of his men from the farm. Somehow, he had managed to shoehorn a whole crew into that roadster. When it came to transport back then, it was a question of getting around by whatever means necessary and just keeping your eyes open for the law along the way. I imagine Father at the wheel, dressed in his collared work shirt, necktie, belt and braces, and with his cap threatening to flip away as he beetled along the byways. It makes me chuckle when I think about all his passengers; squeezed into that three-wheeler with ashen faces while quietly praying he wouldn't corner too quickly.

Having attended to the business at hand, sealing a deal before another buyer got in before him, Father and his crew set their sights on returning to Worcestershire. This time, as he told me, there would be no danger of tipping over or reaching speeds that made their eyes water. In fact, the journey home would take them the best part of a week.

In order to support his contracting business, which depended on this acquisition to grow, my dad intended to bring back a pair of recently retired engines, along with a plough, a scuffle, harrows and a water cart. One of the engines had been stationed on the seafront at Lowestoft and used to haul in mines left over from the First World War. Father was well aware that rust might become an issue on account of the salt water, but then he was as familiar with the inside of those machines as he was with harnessing their muscle. With hard graft, care and commitment, he was certain the pair would provide him with years of service in the fields. That was the beauty of steam power. You could trust it to get the job done.

But first he had to get everything home.

At full speed and on firm, level ground, a steam traction engine will travel at about five to ten miles an hour. You'd barely have to break into a trot to keep up on foot. At the same time, with a steady supply of coal for the firebox and water for the boiler, those machines will just keep on running. As for his crew, Father was mindful that they deserved a good night's rest before embarking on such a gruelling journey.

'We'll stay in town tonight,' he announced, knowing full well that it would bring them some cheer. 'The drinks are on me.'

For men born and bred in rural Worcestershire, who so rarely left the county, the chance to spend a night in a bustling place like Stowmarket would've filled them with excitement. Having checked into their lodgings, no doubt they enjoyed their pub session that night with some gusto. As country folk, it didn't occur to them to safeguard their belongings. Locking doors was just not something they considered, even when leaving behind the money from their pockets to make the most of their boss's generosity, until they wobbled back to discover that someone had rifled through their bags. That was town life for you, they decided, now the gloss and dazzle had deserted them. With dark mutterings of robbers watching their every move, all they could do was fire up their engines at first light and crawl away with their sights set on home.

The way Father told this story, it struck me that just being on the road would've gone some way to restoring his crew's spirit. Under two pillars of billowing steam that joined to form a trail in their wake, one traction engine led the way with the other bringing up the rear and the rest of the tackle in between. Nowadays, with a convoy that long and slow, you would have people blowing their car horns for you to get out of the way. Back then, the roads were mercifully quiet. As if to put the Morgan in its place, in the face of true automotive majesty, my dad hitched the little roadster to the back of the rear engine and towed it homewards.

For the crew, still stung by the robbery, there was no sitting back to admire the landscape. Every man had a role, and while Father took over at the wheel of one of the engines whenever anyone got tired, he had one other vital job. Every now and then, he would hop off the convoy, unhook the Morgan and speed ahead to find sources of water for the ever-thirsty engines. With several days of travel ahead, and thankfully enough money in his wallet to see them all home, Dad was also tasked with seeking out further places to stay. Not only did he have to find somewhere big enough to house his crew, the landlady needed to be fully prepared for the road locomotives that would soon be pulling up outside. All she had to do was listen out, so he said. Such was the noise it would give her plenty of notice.

It wasn't just the steam whistle, which carried for miles around. The rear wheels were huge, wrought from iron, and could cause the ground to rumble. Ultimately, with the promise of so many guests, Father always returned to the convoy having secured a place for them to sleep each night.

And so, after each tough day on the road, the convoy would halt at their stopover and men with soot-blackened clothes and faces would jump to the ground. Mindful to secure their belongings, even in rural stopovers, they'd always end up at a nearby pub. There, over a restorative pint or two, all paid for by my dad, they'd pick over the high points of their travels so far and deliberate what the next day might have in store. Navigating was an art form. Hill climbs could be perilous, while a steady nerve was required on the way down, along with a firm grip on the brake lever. Whatever route the boss chose, however, the men knew they could depend on him. My dad was well aware of the undertaking required in delivering the tools of his trade safely home. A robbery might've overshadowed their departure, but eventually the crew chugged into Inkberrow with smiles on their dirty faces.

For Father, a mounting sense of excitement would have accompanied his relief at delivering both men and machine home in one piece. With the steam tackle at Quarry Pits, he only had the remains of that day to himself, before farm work beckoned once more. Even so, in that short time he made up for the week he had missed.

'I didn't stop thinking about you for a single moment,' he said, standing outside the kitchen door with his week-old daughter in his arms. He was quiet, strong and solid, my dad; weather-beaten much like the house behind him, perhaps, but a family man and always a safe pair of hands. Across the lower fields, crows could be heard settling in as the sun sank away behind the treeline. 'Whatever life has in store for you, little one,' he added, 'this will always be *our* world.'

2

Gentle Giants

Hitching a lift with Father's horse and cart.

I am christened Joan, and nothing more. Mother had three names, but she didn't like to use any of them. Nor was she willing to burden her children with quite so many. Everyone called her Kitty, on account of her being as small as a cat when she was a child, and that suited her just fine.

Marian was born two years before me in the spring of 1930. Although we were both given just one name each, we differed in every other aspect. While she liked to stay indoors and help out in the farmhouse, my interest lay in following my father. She didn't show much interest in the land at that time, or in the potential it had to provide. Even at a young age, I couldn't imagine any other life.

My earliest memory is of trailing after Father as he led his Shire horse and cart out to the fields. It would've been at the crack of dawn, just as the first bars of light reached through the hedgerows and the rooster crowed in the day. He would never wait for me, and I learned quickly to rise and dress before he left the farmhouse. I even took to wearing a necktie so I could look just like him.

I was no more than four years old. All I wanted to do was watch my dad at work. Father also relied upon a loyal band of farm-hands, and they were like family to me. Whatever the weather, I would be there. Whether they were ploughing, planting, harvesting or threshing, working with engines or by hand, I just loved being out in the open air. I would make myself useful wherever I could, which probably didn't amount to much at that age but my enthusiasm surely shone through. The men would share their packed lunch, and talk to me like a grown-up, and I adored every moment. But the best bit, the highpoint of my day, was when it came to heading home. That's when Father would pick me up and plant me on the back of the horse.

'There you are,' he'd say, standing back as if I had just assumed my rightful place.

I was a strikingly small child, with windblown hair when it wasn't tied and a steady gaze at anything that took my interest. What I lacked in stature, however, I made up for in grit. There was nothing on the farm that frightened me, even if I was dwarfed by both machinery and livestock. The Shire horse towered above me as much as the steam traction engines. In some ways, they shared the same temperament. Both were gentle giants, and proved invaluable to us. Riding the engines was always fun, what with the cacophony of pistons, the hissing, whistle and smoke, but it was the horses that proved to be a first love that endured. With Father leading the way, I would do my level best to stay upright; clinging to this majestic and compliant beast as twilight settled over the landscape.

As well as being a blissful time, my fourth year also proved a test for me. At that age, like any child, I was expected to go to school. This meant leaving the sanctuary of Quarry Pits, which was all I knew at the time. By then, my dad's work marked out my days. It helped me to feel secure, and gave me a strong sense of purpose. I couldn't see the point of sitting in a classroom listening to a stranger teach me all these uninteresting, impractical subjects. In my young mind, Father instructed me in everything I would ever need to know in life, and that revolved around the farm. Still, rules were rules. As I was to discover, it meant I had no choice in the matter.

Along with Marian, my sister, I went to a primary school in North Piddle. This was a little parish, bordered to the north by a brook, about four miles away from the farm. By then, with his family growing up, Father had purchased a lovely old Wolseley that would comfortably seat us all. Either he drove us there or we would get a lift with a jolly local farmer called Sidney who also had a child at the school. It meant the journey there was always fun, but that stopped as soon as I walked into the playground. In those early years of my schooling, I would sit at my little wooden desk and look attentive. As the teacher scraped away at the blackboard, however, my thoughts were increasingly elsewhere. Namely back at Quarry Pits, and all the fun, discoveries and the challenges that I believed I was missing. Unlike me, Marian thrived at school. She shone in the classroom and her schoolwork marked her out as someone who might go places. Me? I did as little as I could get away with, and looked forward to the final bell.

As I grew older, and followed Marian to grammar school, so I gained some confidence. Not in my academic abilities but in my determination to follow my heart. I became restless, I suppose; no longer able to just sit there and let it all go over my head. And so one morning I took it upon myself to leave.

'Miss,' I piped up with one hand in the air, and let the expression on my face tell her that I needed to visit the toilet.

It wasn't an unusual request for a pupil to make. No doubt such an interruption irritated my teacher, but she let me go.

My grammar school was in Alcester, a low-lying market town where two rivers converge, almost seven miles east of the farmhouse. I would've been about eleven at the time, and quite capable of walking such a distance. So, skipping past the lavatories, and classes in full swing, I simply left the school building and headed out into the fresh air and the sunshine.

I didn't once question what had been an instinctive decision to leave. Nor did I worry that the head mistress might punish me. All I wanted to do was get back to Quarry Pits and roll up my sleeves to help out. I was still small for my age, and this became even more apparent when my classmates had shot up like weeds. But in the fields I had learned to become a useful pair of hands to my dad. In a way, it made me feel like an equal among his men. Even at that age, I could get stuck in like the rest of the labourers. No doubt they were more effective than me, but Father liked my attitude and the fact that I was always willing to help.

As soon as I got home, I thought to myself, I would change out of my uniform and head down the track to find him. I even began to imagine him reacting with a pleasant surprise when he realised what I had chosen to do.

The route home was lovely and quiet. For a couple of miles, I dawdled along winding country lanes fringed by cow parsley, and just the breeze in the corn for company. It meant I was quick to hear the growl of a car approaching from a long way behind and then slow. I was also familiar with the sound of the engine. Before I stopped and turned around, I just knew that it was Father.

'Get in,' he said, having wound down the window as he drew alongside.

One look at the furrows across his brow told me I was in trouble. Shocked by his bearing, I quickly did as I was told. My heart sank when he found a place to turn the car around and sped back towards Alcester. It didn't take long to return to the school by car, but by God he was fuming. For a man of few words, who could keep a lid on his dismay when a wet season threatened his crops, he knew how to swear when the moment truly seized him. There was nothing I could say to excuse myself or reason with him about my way of thinking. All I could do was sit quietly in the passenger seat and recognise in his mighty rage and cursing that he considered his daughter's education to be more important than anything else. If the school ever raised the alarm again because I had gone missing, he thundered at me, the second most foolish thing I could do would be to show my face at home.

Unfortunately for my dad, even such a dressing down didn't persuade me to sit quietly and follow my sister's example. He might've marched me back into class that day, and left me feeling sorry for myself, but within a short time I had the wind in my sails again.

Something had to be done, Father realised. It didn't matter how many times he ordered me to stay put, the teacher only had to turn her back for a moment before coming back around to find an empty desk.

'What's it going to take?' he grumbled to my mum, Kitty, one time as she simmered a jam mixture on the stove. 'I'd teach her myself but what do I know?'

She turned to face him, with one hand cupped under the spoon that she blew on to cool, and asked him not to worry.

'She'll stay at school,' Mother assured him. 'Don't fret about it any more.'

'How?' he scoffed, but couldn't resist tasting the spoon when she offered it to him.

'Joan knows her own mind all right,' she said, waiting for his nod of approval, 'but she hasn't yet reckoned with me.'

The next day, to my horror, I discovered we had a new pupil in class. She sat there listening attentively to the teacher; upright against the chair back with her shoulders square and both hands clasped politely in her lap. Mother didn't have a desk, however, or exercise books to write in. She just sat so close to me that had I tried to bolt she could've calmly grabbed my wrist. Whenever I caught her eye, she made a circling motion with her finger to direct my attention to the front.

It wasn't just a one-off either. Mother accompanied me to class for a long time after that. Long enough, I suppose, for me to stop huffing and abandon any design on hightailing it home. Like breaking in a horse, she took on a battle of wills with me and won. Eventually, I learned to sit still during school hours and she stopped accompanying me. Even so, my desire to get out into the fields never left me. It was the first thing I did just as soon as school finished every day; joining the others to do my fair share until the light had left the sky.

By rights, I should've stayed in education until I turned fourteen. I began to look forward to reaching that age with every day that passed. Even though I'd sometimes be required to stay off school, if we were planting corn and Dad needed the help, I'd still be expected to return to the classroom as soon as possible. While Marian excelled, and continued her schooling, all I could do was focus on not fidgeting until it was time to grab my satchel and go. Then, with a year left before I could officially leave, Mother fell ill. As she took to her bed to recover, both Marian and I were required back at Quarry Pits. While my sister managed both the cooking and cleaning duties, I helped out with the farm-hands and Father didn't once complain. Nor did he order me to follow Marian back to school when Mother recovered her health. We never discussed it, in fact, but having come into my own I knew that phase of my life was behind me at last. I had earned my place in the fields now. And nothing, I believed, would ever take me away from that again.

3

Brother John

Brother John and some of the farm-hands who helped us.

Towards the end of 1936, just after I had started my schooling, my brother came into the world. For a farming family, the arrival of a boy was often considered to be an extra cause for celebration. It meant as he grew up he could be put to good use.

Sure enough, John would follow in our father's footsteps and become a respected farmer in his own right. Naturally, my mum and dad were overjoyed at his safe delivery but his gender made no odds. By then, I was already spending most of my time with the cattle and the crops. In a sense, they already had a boy.

The arrival of a third and final sibling in the Collins clan would come to make things easier between Marian and me. We loved each other as family, but it's fair to say that we really didn't have that much in common. Just as I could always be found outside, working with Father and his men, my sister was a home-maker like Mother. From an early age she learned to cook and darn and clean, and clearly took great pride in her work. Maybe she simply didn't like it when I returned to the farmhouse covered in muck. She'd never dare say anything to our dad, of course, but Marian liked to put me in my place when our parents' backs were turned.

'What you need,' she said to me one day when I was no more than five, 'is a haircut.'

She announced this at the door to the bedroom we shared, clutching a pair of scissors from Mother's sewing box. I looked up at her from the linoleum floor and wondered why she was taking such a close interest in me.

'But I like my hair,' I told her, and shook out my long golden ringlets. Everyone admired its colour and spring, so I was in no hurry to change it. 'I'm fine just as I am, thank you.'

Marian considered me from the doorframe. She was a tall and broad-shouldered child, approaching nine at the time, and wasn't shy in bossing me about. I could handle Shire horses, and the clank of a traction engine never startled me, but my sister's physical size and sheer force of will could make her hard to reckon with. With a gleam in her eye, she opened the scissors and snapped them shut again.

'I'll make you look pretty,' she promised, and stepped into my room.

Sometimes, if Marian didn't get her own way, she was known to pinch and scratch. So, when she asked me to pull out a chair and sit on it I did as I was told. She cut my hair with no mirror, and faced me towards the window overlooking the fields on the other side of the lane. As my locks fell into my lap, I just stared through the glass and listened to her coo how beautiful I would be once she'd finished. Working methodically, stepping around me with each snip until she'd gone full circle, Marian stepped back and beamed at me.

'There,' she said. 'What would you do without me?'

Well, I didn't know what to make of it. At that age, I just accepted my sister's word and got on with my day. It was only when I skipped downstairs and found my mother in the kitchen that I realised Marian might've taken me for a fool.

Even for a pudding bowl cut, my sister had done a bad job. She'd literally hacked around my head and over my ears until I looked dramatically different. Mother was so annoyed that day, but Marian never got into big trouble for it. She always seemed to get away with things, which was down to the fact that we'd nearly lost her once from appendicitis. From that moment on, she couldn't do much wrong in my parents' eyes, though my haircut certainly tested them. That day, Father had been out overseeing the transport of his steam tackle to work on another farm. When he walked through the kitchen door, and found my sister and I looking downcast and tearful, he simply stared at me while listening to Marian explain herself.

'Joan acts like a boy,' she said in her defence, as Mother looked on from behind us while nursing the new baby. 'So I gave her a boy's haircut.'

Marian and I might've been very different in spirit, but we adored our brother John equally. He took after Father in so many ways. Physically, he shared the same solid frame, sparrow-brown hair and a level gaze that could size you up in a second. Like Dad, his mouth could tighten in pride as much as indignation, but it took a great deal before he expressed himself in words.

Brother was also good with his hands. A practical lad, he liked to build his own toys out in the barn across the courtyard from the house. Naturally, being surrounded by the genuine article, he was drawn to making steam tractors. Our John would use whatever he could to make the body and wheels, from oil drums to wooden pallets, before hammering and binding it all together. His engines were wonderful. He'd spend hours at work on them, and then climb on board to fire up the boilers in his imagination. But if his pretend engines ever failed on him, and something would always come loose or fall off, we would see another side to his character that he must've inherited from Dad. It was as if he just couldn't handle seeing his hard work come undone, and that's when his temper took over. Goodness, it was a transformation. This freckle-faced little boy, dressed in a shirt, shorts and braces, could shout and stomp about. Generally, however, he expressed his rage by kicking his creations into bits. He'd calm down in his own time, withdrawing from the world for a little bit, and then return ready to take on the next task.

As well as building pretend engines, John shared my enthusiasm for watching Dad's men at work on the real thing. As soon as he was old enough, he would join me on the dawn plod out to the field. It was such a beautiful time of day, with the sun reaching over the horizon and birdsong in the air. John would always stick close by, not least because I knew enough by then to explain just what was involved in ploughing a field by steam power. While the farm-hands prepared to start work, often five or six of them silhouetted by the strengthening sun as they clambered over the engines, I would stand there with my little mate and provide a running commentary.

'Just wait for the whistle, Brother,' I always said. 'One toot to pull, and two to stop.'

On land like ours at Quarry Pits – heavy, clotted stuff that could scupper a steam tractor if it attempted to cross – Fowler engines served as the most effective form of ploughing. Named after the engineer who had worked to solve the challenge faced by farmers like us, two were needed to make the system work. Having claimed such a pair from service on the seafront, pulling in mines from the ocean, Father and his men would position the Fowlers side on to one another at opposing headlands of the field. Each one was fitted with a rotating winch drum between the front and rear axle, and linked by heavy steel cable. Despite his tender years, John would always want to join the farm-hands in hauling it across the field for the hook-up.

'I can help,' he'd say. 'Just watch.'

Like me at that age, my brother was enthusiastic even if his contribution had yet to prove useful. He'd scamper alongside the men as they dragged the cable across, and then watch closely when they secured a steam-driven plough at one end. This was designed with two sets of blades on a see-saw frame so it could work in both directions. Next, with every man tasked with a job, the boilers would be filled from the water cart, which travelled everywhere with them, and the fireboxes in both engines stoked up to temperature. This could have taken a couple of hours beforehand, and demanded calm, patience and careful balancing of heat and pressure. To make the most of the daylight, the crews would often light the coals before dawn. When working the fields over a period of days, some even slept in wagons attached to the engines.

Once the Fowlers were ready to come alive, the foreman would talk to the crew on the other with a shrill burst of the steam whistle. Like birdsong, it was simply part of the landscape. I also knew it was time to make sure that John and I were standing back at a safe distance.

'Are you ready?' I'd ask, as his hand found mine and we'd watch the next stage play out.

With the pistons chugging into life on the hauling engine, and the drums rotating, one hundred and fifty feet of steel cable took up the slack. Spooling off one drum, and winding onto the other, this low-slung tight rope began to tighten and then move. From the other side of the field, as the plough lurched towards the engine at a steady walking pace, a farm-hand perched on a seat at the back would keep it straight and locked true in the furrows. A flagman would often accompany him to relay signals, for communication was vital at all times, and so the work would begin. Some ploughs could manage six furrows at a time, which took some concentration. Once it reached the end, the width of the drum on the Fowler allowed the crew to move the plough across and tip the frame so the other blades bit into the ground. When the implement was in position, the farm-hand would swap seats and tackle the next line of furrows. Finally, both machines would inch forward on their giant wheels so the process could be repeated across the field.

Incredibly, with a dependable crew, it was possible to cover twenty acres in a single day. The work was tough, hot, dirty and laborious. There was also something rhythmical and poetic about it. Standing in the field as the plough sails past, all you can hear is the rattle and patter of the blades cutting through the soil and the odd stone skittering, which is why my little brother and I had to keep out of the way. Even from a distance, the sound is eerie, relentless and strangely calming. It's an unforgettable experience and an art form in some ways. It was also a way of life for my father, Colin Collins, just as it would become for John and me.

While Marian proved herself to be quite the scholar, Dad found himself with another problem schoolchild on his hands. I might've proved to be a restless soul in the classroom. John just turned out to be a nightmare. Shortly after starting school, Brother must've done something so unspeakable that he was sent packing. The head mistress just couldn't handle him, and he ended up back at the farmhouse under the watchful eye of a private tutor.

My parents were only trying to do right by him. Unfortunately, in deciding that home schooling was the appropriate option for John, they overlooked the fact that he was closer to temptation than I ever was in the classroom. It didn't take much. Just the sound of a steam whistle as the Fowler crews worked on the fields, and Brother reacted like he'd lost all self-restraint. One moment, his tutor would be guiding him through the basics of algebra, the next, a distant toot would prompt him onto his feet with his exercise books in hand.

'Sit back down this minute!' he'd be told, but it was too late for all that. Instead of bowing to authority, and with a defiant look in his eye, our John would fling his work from the open window before hightailing it out to the fields. In the same way that Mother had worked on breaking me, our parents persevered with John. In the end, they found a way to open his eyes and ensured that he received a good schooling. At the same time, our mum and dad fully recognised that on the farm he was in his element. There was no hint of mischief or insurrection from him out there. John knew he'd found his calling, as did I, and by the time we'd each turned eight Father considered us to be part of his crew.

We weren't just brother and sister, John and me. Growing up at Quarry Pits, we were best friends, and the most hardworking young farm-hands you ever did meet.

4

Loyalty and Love

A Hereford heifer at Quarry Pits.

From an early age, I had a keen understanding that animals could be a vital source of labour. Our horses never complained at the loads that they had to haul, and when it came to light ploughing they were as important to my dad as the Fowler engines were for the heavier work. The livestock also provided an income, of course. Up to sixty cattle could be grazing on the pasturelands at Quarry Pits, mostly bred for beef, but also milk and butter. Father always kept a couple of pigs as well, which served as living ploughs in their own right. Then there were the two hen houses behind the barn. They could hold up to one thousand birds each, either Rhode Island Reds or Sussex Whites, and Mother made sure they produced a small profit. Like Father, she knew that every penny counts in keeping a farm afloat, and both were keen to pass on that understanding to their children. But during my upbringing at Quarry Pits, above all else, I learned that animals could also represent qualities that would come to define my life over the years: independence, loyalty and love.

Inside the farmhouse, Mother had two sources of great pride. The kitchen was her kingdom. She kept the dresser and the quarry tiles clean and polished at all times, and would conjure up mouth-watering stews and delicious cakes from the Aga. But Kitty Collins also devoted her time to another pursuit. Twice a day, she would break away from cooking and cleaning to busy herself in a room on the other side of the house. The door was kept shut at all times, to keep the warmth inside at a steady temperature. For this room contained her incubator: a solid wooden cabinet so big and imposing it looked like the farmhouse had been built around it. Heated by paraffin-fired lamps, the contraption took up so much space that you had to squeeze around the outside, and was fitted with racks that could hold a thousand eggs at a time.

'Work surely and gently, and keep a watchful eye,' said Mother, once she had taught me how to help her, for the task required a lot of concentration. With so many eggs, brought in from the sheds, I quickly learned how to tell if any were close to hatching. Sometimes, I'd have to press my thumb gently against the shell to help the chick inside break free. At busy times, towards the end of a cycle and especially if the incubator was close to full, it could take a while to work our way around. Slowly, the sound of cheeping would fill the room. Having sexed them, the hatched chicks went into one of two boxes: one for pullets and the other for cockerels, before both went off to market.

As a little girl, helping out in the incubator room was just another job to be done on the farm. I learned to be careful and kind, of course, but never looked after the chicks for long enough to feel a lasting bond.

The dogs in my life were a different story. We always had some on the farm. Mother bred Old English Sheepdogs, and she was very good at it, too. These big, shaggy pups were so playful and friendly, and I was always very sorry when the time came for them to go to new homes. Father kept working dogs, like Mick the collie. Then there was Punch, who never liked to be alone. He would follow him out to work, watch Mum cooking in the kitchen, or play with John and me. I remember that dog fondly, because he helped me out whenever I failed to clear my plate at suppertime. Dad was a stickler for the rules, and so if I'd been picking at berries all afternoon and couldn't finish my meal, he'd send me to his office to eat alone.

'Don't come out until that plate is clean,' he'd say, and order me to leave the table.

All I had to do was glance at Punch and he would know what was in store. That dog would slip out after me, and even get ahead as I crossed the corridor to Dad's office. Once inside, I'd set my plate on the floor and be free to leave within a minute at most.

'There!' I'd declare, and hold a plate up so spotless that Mother could've served another meal on it.

In time, Dad cottoned on to what I was doing. You couldn't slip much past him. But he never once got angry with me about it. I even wondered if he was coming round to the fact that his sec-ond-born daughter always rose to a challenge.

Punch was the first dog to help me out of a scrape. Years later, it was my turn to come to the assistance of a dog that meant so much to me. We hadn't intended to take in Fido. He was just one of those lost souls who found a home with us. I discovered him by chance one day; a sorry-looking spaniel cowering in the under-growth out by the yard.

'Hello, you!' I said, dropping down to get a closer look. The dog had wriggled deep into the tangle of thorns and nettles. I reached out a hand, and he growled at me. I was scared he'd bite me, of course, but I could see from its bearing that the dog was more frightened than me. So I just kept my distance and talked soothingly. It was in pain. That was clear. And when I summoned Dad he pointed out that the pads on its paws were raw and bleeding.

'He's been abandoned,' he said with some certainty. 'Someone has driven him far from home and then left the poor sod. The road surface does that to a dog. They just run and run, desperate to catch up with their owner, until they can't run any further.'

Father left me in the yard with my heart in my mouth. How could someone abandon any dog, I wondered? There and then, I resolved to take him in. But first I had to gain his trust.

Food seemed like the surest way to win him over. I swiped some scraps from the kitchen into a bowl and left it at the edge of the undergrowth. Two hunted brown eyes locked on to my offering, but the spaniel didn't move, and so I retreated inside. A few hours later, I crept out to find the dog was in the same place, but all the food had gone.

'You're doing the right thing,' said Mother, when I returned with the empty bowl.

'How long will it take?' I asked.

She smiled and took the bowl from me.

'Just don't give up on him, Joan,' she said, though I didn't need to be told.

It took a week, leaving out food at dusk and dawn, before that dog braved feeding from my hand. That was all it took for a bond to form. I had to carry the poor thing into the farmhouse and dress his injured paws, but he never tried to get away. Fido made a full recovery, in body and spirit, and though he liked to sleep out at night, he was always there for me. The dog would often curl up beside a wall that housed a curious little statue of a child. Nobody quite knew what purpose the statue served, or who had removed the brick to install it and then encased it with a plate of glass. I sometimes wondered whether Fido had chosen that spot because he liked to feel that someone was watching over him, or whether he felt a duty to look out for the child.

While the dogs provided our family with companionship, and Mother supplemented the household income with her chicks, it was Dad who decided that I should learn the true value of a live-stock animal. One day, he led me down to the holding yard with the promise of a surprise. I just stood there staring at the calf, and then looked up at him.

'She's all yours,' he announced, standing with me behind the gate.

'Take care of her, and in a few years from now she'll fetch you good money.'

'Do you mean it?' I asked.

'Every farmer has to start somewhere.' Father ruffled my hair with his hand. 'This is where you begin.'

The calf that Dad had singled out for me was a Hereford heifer, with that characteristic red body and a white switch from her face to her chest. A breed raised by and large for meat production, this was the cattle of choice at Quarry Pits, and Father had entrusted one to me. Naturally, I took my responsibilities very seriously. As a small girl, however, growing up around carthorses and nurturing a passion for ponies, I also hatched other designs for that young heifer.

'Her name is Nimrod,' I told John, having led them both out to the field. Somehow, I had encouraged the heifer to bite down on a bridle, and saddled her up with an old sack held in place with a strap. 'Here,' I said, and offered John the reins. 'Hold this while I climb on.'

For her breed, Nimrod was a compliant beast. She stood calmly at the gate, which I had to clamber up so I could mount her, and didn't complain when I picked up the reins. Not that she had any sense of what I was asking her to do, of course. Even though that little calf remained rooted to the spot, Brother and I were determined.

Between us, taking turns on her back, we transformed Nimrod into a championship horse in our minds. Eventually, with a lot of encouragement and some heaving, we even persuaded that young Hereford to move. Maybe she was just shifting from one patch of grass to another at first, but in time we could instruct her to trot. Well, the sight of us two kids on her back must've raised a few smiles, and said a great deal about our perseverance. Unfortunately, after a few months, we could no longer pretend that Nimrod was destined to become a championship show jumper. As a sexually maturing heifer, with hormones beginning to course through her system, her interests turned to the bull in the nearby field. The last thing she wanted, with mating in mind, was for two children to take her by the reins and ride her around.

It didn't take long for John and I to recognise that Nimrod was best left to graze in peace. We only had to throw the sack over her back for her to bolt and buck, and show the kind of temper that persuaded us both to retreat to the safe side of the gate. Still, I raised that heifer as Father expected.

Three years after he had given me a calf of my own, I led a healthy adult Hereford to market and earned a good sum for my efforts. I also knew exactly what I wanted to put the money towards. Nimrod might not have been the best horse a girl could wish for, or even a horse at all, but she had kindled an interest in riding that has never left me. And so with that money in my pocket, along with the chance to raise another calf thanks to the generosity of my dad, I resolved that one day I would make my dreams come true.

Like so many young girls, I'd set my heart on a pony. I once tried to make do with a donkey, but that didn't work out very well. John and I took her out for a ride one time, but she just laid down on the lane. Refusing to budge, she blocked the traffic for a whole hour. By then, I knew that only the genuine article would do. Once I'd saved up enough money, I pestered Father to let me buy one. He gave in once I pointed out that a pony could pull a small plough, which was perfect for turning the mangle field down on the low ground. For once, school served a useful purpose, because that's where I learned my friend, Edna, had a tan and white piebald for sale. Sparks was her name, and I soon discovered that it summed up her nature. She was a lively thing, but by then I had scrabbled together enough time in the saddle to know what I was doing. Together with my brother, John, who rode beside me on his bicycle, we would head off down the lanes at the weekends to ride in local gymkhanas. I won plenty of rosettes in my day, and no doubt that boosted my confidence. Of course, riding has a painful way of reminding you not to lose your head. One time I was galloping along the upper edge of the fields on the ridge when a stork flew out of the hedgerow. Sparks reared up and threw me off, before finding her own way home.

When I came to my senses, sometime later, I returned to find my family had sent out search parties. The next day, my much-relieved Father set out to buy me a riding hat. They weren't commonplace in those days, and he had to drive all the way to London to find one.

'Joan, I recognise there's no stopping you,' he said, having encouraged me back in the saddle. 'Just promise me you'll be careful.'

'Don't worry,' I assured him, and tapped my new headgear.

Father stood back and flattened his lips.

'I can't afford for you to have another accident,' he said, and spread his great hands. 'Who will help me in the fields?'

And so, with my new hat strapped on tight, I quickly regained my confidence with Sparks and just took off across country. I adored the sense of freedom, in the same way I imagine Father relished his time behind the wheel of his roadster. It was in complete contrast to the slow, steady and methodical work with the steam ploughs, which I loved in equal measure.

5

'Ain't Got a Boy at All

Working the thresher was a tiring job.

Being as small as a bird set me apart from others in several ways. It meant I was good for some tasks that required a nimble little frame. I liked to feel as if I could be helpful, but I wasn't so happy about what it meant in some other respects. Bath nights were a case in point. When I was a child, Dad fitted a back boiler behind the Aga range. He plumbed the whole house, in fact, which meant that we could draw hot water upstairs. Well, not everyone in the family enjoyed such a luxury …

In the Collins family, we had a pecking order. With the tub filled, Mother would climb in first for a soak, and then Dad took his turn. Working with steam traction engines, he'd often return home looking more like a coal miner surfaced from the pits. As a result, the bath water that awaited his children would be black and with a layer of grit upon the bottom. Being the eldest child, Marian was next, and I never quite worked out why John sometimes jumped in before me. It just meant that when I finally had the bath to myself, the water would be tepid at best. What's more, I could sometimes climb out feeling grubbier than when I'd braved getting in.

Even on those occasions when I was lucky enough to come out feeling scrubbed and fresh, it rarely lasted long. There were just so many jobs to be done around the farm that involved getting mucky. Because of my size, every year I was tasked with the dirtiest job of them all. It might come as a surprise when I say that it was one that didn't even require me to leave the farmhouse.

'It's that time again,' Father said, on his knees in front of the fireplace in the central bedroom. Peering up the chimney, he reached up towards a ventilation brick at the back and then came away to show me his blackened fingertips. 'I'd ask the sweep but he charges so much for the flues as it is.'

'I'm ready,' I said, and tied back my hair.

I was already in my work clothes, which would soon be unfit for anything but a hot wash. Father caught my eye and smiled fondly.

'You know I'd do it myself if I could,' he said, which made me chuckle, for it must've been years since he'd been able to carry out the task I faced.

Fitted wardrobes flanked the fireplace in that bedroom. Inside the wardrobe closest to the window, if you got on your hands and knees and cleared out the shoes and boxes, you'd find a cubby hole at the back. It was a squeeze, but with a bit of wriggling I could access the void behind the fireplace. Crouched inside that space, I would then take the lamp that Dad passed through to me before looking up and around. He never explained why the void was there, but I suppose it had something to do with the circulation of air. Needless to say it was choked with soot, and my role was to clean it. By any measure, that was one mucky job. I'd be in there for ages, scraping, brushing and scrubbing until it was fit for another twelve months.

I imagine while I was labouring away, Father must've stood in the bedroom and hoped that his little girl wouldn't grow up too quickly. For my small size didn't just mark me out for useful chores inside the farmhouse. As my dad discovered at the end of a long and challenging day, there was one vital job when it came to maintaining the traction engines that none of his men could manage as well as me.

Father owned a lot of steam tackle, and not just for ploughing but threshing as well. Like any heavy agricultural machinery, repair work took up a great deal of his time. There was always something that needed fixing, welding or replacing, either in the workshop, out on the fields or on site at another farm that had leased engines from him. Naturally, I went along with him whenever I could. I had a hunger to learn how everything worked. I was also lucky enough that my dad was willing to show me. We were a team, Father and I, and sometimes that would come as a shock to people.

'Fetch me a five-eight spanner, will you?' he asked me once. We were out at Frank John's farm. He had summoned Dad because one of the plough concaves had broken and needed to be replaced. We had driven over in the Wolseley, parked up on the lane and then trudged along a muddy track to find the crew standing idle. Any kind of breakdown can cost a farmer dearly, especially if the weather is against them. With the men watching Dad as he wrestled to free the concave, I sensed many eyes turn in my direction when he asked me for that tool.

'A five-eight?' scoffed one young lad, a new pair of hands by the name of Rex Jackson. 'What does a little girl know about spanners?'

As Dad kept a lot of his tools in the car for call-outs, I had just turned to head back down the track at the time. I caught Rex's eye as I passed by, and noted the half-smile on his face. My dad, however, found nothing funny about the situation.

'Master Jackson,' he said. 'If I send Joan for a five-eight spanner then she will bring me one.'

I knew exactly where to find it, and held my head up high when

I returned. Rex Jackson never cast doubt on me again, and treated me just like any other farm-hand. I adored my dad in lots of ways, but I loved best that he would stand up for me if anyone cast doubt on my abilities. In fact, it sometimes seemed to me that he would've preferred it if every man who worked for him was a little bit more like me.

'If you got a boy, then you got a boy,' he was famous for saying whenever his farm-hands were caught fooling around in numbers. 'If you got two boys, then you only have half a boy,' he went on, before a smile eased across his face. 'And if you got three boys, then you 'ain't got a boy at all.'

In me, he had a daughter dressed in lad's clothing. A tomboy, if you like. I just got stuck in like everyone else, and people respected me for it. The men had even taken to calling me 'Mr Collins' boy girl', and I didn't mind one bit. So long as I got to do my fair share of work, I was happy. And if there were a task to be done that nobody else could do, I would be in my element.

One job that nobody relished involved the engine boilers. These were big old vessels, like giant kettles, and prone to lime scale. On a regular basis, they would need cleaning, which was no easy job. Like the void behind the fireplace at the farmhouse, it required someone to climb into a confined space with a hammer and a limitless pot of elbow grease. I suppose the farm-hands could be forgiven for thinking it was a man's job. That was just how it could be in those days. Now the boiler hatch on every engine was small and oval-shaped. That ruled out many of the men on account of their size, including Father. One time, during a spring-clean of the steam tackle, the task fell to a rangy farm-hand called George who was new to the crew. It was an unseasonably hot day, and many of the crew had removed the shirts from their backs. The young man nominated to squeeze inside had already worked up a sweat, which my dad regarded as a good thing.

'The slippier you are the better,' he joked, as the men gave him a leg up to the hatch. 'You'll squeeze inside in no time.'

It wasn't easy, fitting through that hatch. I watched George go in head first, cupping my brow against the sun as he struggled to ease his shoulders through.

'*Heave!*' The men joked as they helped him along. '*Ho!*'

Waist deep, George suddenly slipped from view as if hauled in from the inside of the boiler. The men cheered, laughing among themselves as one tossed in the hammer so he could chip away at the furring. Father shoved a box under the hatch so he could stand on it to look in. Peering through the opening, he addressed George as if his name were a question in itself.

'Time to start work, lad,' he added after a moment. 'There's a lot to be done.'

'*I can't,*' came the small voice in reply, which quickly quelled the chatter. '*I'm sorry, Sir.*'

'Are you hurt?' Dad rocked up onto his toes for a better look inside. 'Speak up, George! What's the matter?'

'*I don't like it in here,*' came the reply. '*I … I'm very scared.*'

Of course, this earned him some jibes from his crew at the foot of the engine, but Father was quick to hush them. Having worked all his life with steam tackle, he had a strong sense of responsibility for the men who worked for him. He also had some sense that it could be suffocating inside those boilers in different ways.

'You're quite safe,' he assured him. 'Nothing bad can happen, lad. Just pick up the hammer and you'll be out in no time.'

Standing with the farm-hands behind my dad I held my breath and listened out for a response. It was little more than a whimper, muffled by his confines, but we heard it loud and clear.

The boy had suffered a fright. It had never occurred to me to be scared whenever I crawled into the void behind the fireplace, but I could understand the fear that gripped him. It wasn't just the darkness in there but the confines of the space. Unless you focused on the task at hand, and trusted those on the other side to get you out, I suppose it would be quite easy to become spooked. It was just before lunch, and this was the last task before we broke to eat.

Once it became clear to Father that the lad was frozen with fear, and mindful that mutterings of frustration might make things worse, he dismissed his men to enjoy their sandwiches in the sun.

'Come out whenever you're ready,' he told the boy, and stepped down to join me. 'Joan and I won't leave you, will we, Gal?'

'No, sir,' I said, and grinned when he winked at me.

As it turned out, that lunch break lasted long into the afternoon. Father kept talking to the lad, seeking to ease his fears and coax him out, but nothing would get through to him. Having squeezed his way through the hatch, poor George was now gripped by a fear of constriction. Exasperated, my dad let me peer through the hatch to speak to him. In the weak light, dimmed further by my head at the hatch, I saw George bunched up on the boiler floor with his arms wrapped tight around his legs and a blank look on his face.

'Would you care for a sandwich? I asked. George made no response. 'How about some company?' I offered instead, and grasped the hatch as if preparing to clamber through.

'Don't!' he said, out of nowhere, it seemed. I looked back down to see his pale, tear-streaked face peering up at me. 'It wouldn't do for two of us to be trapped in here forever.'

'But you can do it,' I insisted, and extended my hand. 'Come on, George. I'll guide you all the way.'

In accessing the fireplace void, as I explained to him just then, I had learned to wriggle with my shoulder blades. It wasn't a pleasant sensation when midway through a tight gap, and it often felt as though I might get stuck fast, but determination and a bit of courage always saw me through.

'I can't,' he said again, but by now I held his gaze and had no intention of letting it go.

'I'm not scared,' I told him with a mischievous glint in my eye. 'And I'm just a girl.'

George responded with a blink, as if perhaps a spell had been broken before his eyes. And there, together with Father, we coaxed that young man back into the sunshine. I talked him through how to hold himself like a foetus in breech, while Dad kept his mind focused on all the good things that awaited him (sparing his curses over all the lost hours for when the working day had ended). George came out with a pop, like a birth in some ways, and promptly wailed with his first gasp of fresh air. It was a relief for everyone, but that still left a boiler in dire need of descaling.

And with the blessing of my father, who would go on to tell his crew that he would rather lose four of his men than me, I took the hammer and clambered back up to the hatch.

Working away inside those confines, I refused to allow myself to be gripped by the same looming dread that had struck that poor lad. However, towards the tail-end of that decade, a sense that something very bad was closing in began to affect not just our life at Quarry Pits but the nation as a whole.

6

Lights Out

In the timber yard with Harry Taylor and David Hughes.

Dad was a Churchill man. He'd sit before the wireless and listen to each speech with an expression that was focused and increasingly grave. All I understood from the rousing voice that addressed us over the airwaves, and from the long conversations my parents would share, was that our lives were set to change dramatically.

Throughout the Second World War, Colin Collins was required to continue working at Quarry Pits. As a farmer with one hundred acres of agricultural land, his role was to contribute to the feeding of the British people at a time of rationing and hardship. It was a responsibility he took very seriously indeed. At the same time, every man of fighting age who worked for him had been called up. It left Father with the same tasks through every day, week, month and season, but with a smaller, older crew to rely upon. Naturally, his work became even more of a challenge. As a family, it meant we were required to pull together like never before.

At the time, I was struck by how dark life became on our farm.

Not just in a figurative sense, with so many familiar farm-hands gone and rationing beginning to bite, but literally in the measures we had to take during the blackout.

'Joan, take yourself outside and check the windows,' Mother would say to me at dusk. We had already been around every room inside the farmhouse, drawing all the blinds and closing every curtain tight, but my role was to see if any light might still be seeping through. With a threat from the air, we had been warned that any visible landmark on the ground could guide the German bombers to their destination. Even more immediately, as my dad warned, with so much of the countryside enshrouded in darkness it would take just one rogue lamp for a bomber to perfect his target practice.

My mum was a thorough woman, as evident in her work with the great incubator. But if a chink of light should escape her efforts to black out the farmhouse, I was expected to tap on the glass or point to the source so that she and Marian could attend to it. When we had finished, I would head back inside and hope that I hadn't missed anything. This was a nightly chore, which we carried out with painstaking care. Even then, however, nobody ever felt quite safe. Living in a rural landscape, surrounded by fields and woodland, it was easy to think the dark unnatural footprint of a dwelling like a farmhouse could be distinguished from the night sky. In a sense, there was nowhere to hide.

Unlike the towns, we had no electricity at Quarry Pits but a plentiful supply of paraffin lamps. Moving around the farmhouse with a lamp in hand would cause shadows to creep or leap across the walls, and that movement would always come alive in my imagination. At such a young age, the enemy had no face. It just represented something I didn't want to think about: a disruption to a world of my own that I had come to cherish. Even in bed, tucked up under the blankets, I would lie there wondering what might happen to us all.

Of course, there wasn't much time to stew and fret during the days. We had too much work to do in keeping the farm up and running. Each morning, for my first task, I had to get up before the dawn chorus to help Father milk the cows. John would sometimes hear me rising and scramble out of bed so that he could come with me. Often it would still be dark outside, and pitch black inside the milking shed. To help us out, still mindful of the precautions we were expected to take, our dad took some of the paraffin lamps and coated the glass shades in paint. It was a good idea from a practical-minded man. Unfortunately, he painted the shades so thickly that the lamps emitted barely any light at all. It meant all three of us were forced to milk by touch as much as by hand, which resulted in quite a lot of muttering and spilled pails, not to mention hushed laughter.

There wasn't much to smile about then, but Dad still liked to tell us stories as we worked that would keep our spirits up. I remember one tale he shared under those pale lamplights. It had happened, so he told us, in the early years after he took over the running of Quarry Pits from his father.

'One of the neighbouring farm-hands fell in love with the drink,' he said. 'He'd be weaving and wobbling on the job sometimes, and so I decided to teach him a lesson.'

'What did you do?' asked John.

Dad paused in his milking, pushed his cap back up his brow and chuckled.

'I unhooked his horse from the trap when he wasn't looking,' he said, 'and then hooked it back up again through the bars of a gate.'

I laughed at the picture he then painted in our minds of him locking the gate and then hiding in the barn to see what happened.

'Did he work it out?' I asked.

'The poor fellow didn't even come close!' Father spread his hands. 'He was there for an hour at least, staggering around trying to work out what was stopping the cart from moving every time he tried to lead the horse away. When I popped out and solved his problem, he just look baffled before riding off without even a thank you!'

Listening to our dad's tales in the gloom, laughing at his antics, it struck me that he knew how important it was to bring some light into our lives at that time. It took some getting used to in those early days of the conflict. Still, I tried to make myself as useful as I could. There was much that went beyond my capabilities, of course, but where possible he would involve me, and even come to rely on my presence. We worked hard until the sun went down, when there was little more that we could do outside. Then we'd retreat inside the farmhouse once again like rabbits to a burrow. We never locked the door, however. It just wasn't something that we ever felt the need to do. What's more, with only an outside privy for a toilet there would always come a time in the night when each and every one of us would have to answer the call of nature.

'You can take a candle if you must,' Mother would say to me, on nights when there was no moon or stars visible in the sky. 'Just be quick and put it out at once should you hear *anything*.'

The privy was a narrow little outbuilding that was hidden away at the far end of the garden. From the kitchen door, you took the path alongside the farmhouse and then followed it across the grass between borders of blue lilacs. The privy housed two latrine pits side by side: one big and one small. I could only use the small pit. Being so little, there was always a danger that I might fall clean through the other one. During the blackout, however, my biggest fear wasn't the cesspool below ground but the threat from above.

As soon as I cracked open the kitchen door, ready to answer the call of nature, I'd sense my heartbeat quicken. Growing up in the countryside, I wasn't scared of the dark at all. Even so, when I padded out in my nightgown during that time, and made my way along the path, I did so with bated breath. In my young mind, that candle in my hand must've shone so brightly, like a beacon that could be seen for miles around. Were Jerry to be flying around up there, looking for somewhere to drop their bombs, surely they'd have me in their sights within a blink. That thought was certainly enough for me to pick up my pace, though I needn't have worried. Where the path extended beyond the corner of the farmhouse, a small cross-breeze from across the fields would always catch me. Even in calm conditions, it was enough to blow out the candle flame. And on an overcast night, with no light peeping through the curtains from the farmhouse, I would be left blind and disorientated.

With all manner of fears unfurling in my mind, I would sometimes have to rely on the feel of the lilacs to guide me across the garden. Even having reached the relative solace of the privy, and closed the door behind me, my ordeal continued. For sometimes I would have no way of knowing whether I was settling over the little latrine or the large one, which I feared might swallow me whole if I lost my footing. It was a question of keeping my nerve throughout and then focusing on getting back to the farmhouse as calmly, silently and swiftly as I could. Any noise or dawdling, I thought to myself, might alert the enemy.

At Quarry Pits after dark, it's common to hear the distant cry of a fox, a dog barking from a neighbouring farm or the rustle caused by some nocturnal creature as it scrabbles into the undergrowth. It leaves you keenly aware of any sound that might not seem in keeping with that world. The first time I heard what would become a familiar drone, it seemed to reach out over the night sky and proved impossible to pinpoint. Like an unseen swarm of bees, it was an inescapable and malevolent presence. On hearing those bombers I'd catch my breath and then just run for the kitchen door.

Even back inside the farmhouse, among my family once more, I never felt entirely safe. We'd sit together, Mum, Dad, Marian, John and I, sometimes without breathing a word. With the paraffin lamps extinguished, all we could do was listen and hope for the best as the planes passed overhead.

'They're gone for now,' Father would say eventually, and light up a lamp once more. His face in that light would always be strongly contrasted. It made him easy to read no matter how much he reassured us all that everything would be fine. 'Let's pray for those who might not be so fortunate.'

The Luftwaffe had set their sights on Birmingham and other industrial towns near us such as Coventry; some thirty miles to the north east. Dad always told my little brother that we would not be targets, but nobody could be certain where the bombs would drop. Often, after an air raid, the Luftwaffe would simply shed the last of their loads over the countryside at random before hightailing it for the Channel. It was these moments that left everyone in the area fearful for their lives.

One night a bomb must've detonated in nearby woods, because the force of the explosion could be felt through the house. Thankfully nobody was injured. In fact, the damage only served to strengthen our resolve. Mother made the discovery a few days after the strike. She was on her way out to tend to the hen houses when she noticed the glass encasing the little statue of the child had shattered and fallen away. It had been fine the day before, and so she could only conclude that the blast had knocked it out. The statue, however, remained intact, which both my parents considered to be a good omen.

'He's taking a stand against Jerry,' joked Dad. 'And we should follow his example.'

7

The War Ag

Driving a tractor aged sixteen.

Growing up on a farm, I soon learned that if someone shows up in a suit it spells trouble.

'Is your father here, child? May we have a word?'

I was in the yard, untangling a ball of binder twine, when they came. I heard the sound of a vehicle pulling up at the top of the slope, followed by doors opening and closing. The dog went off to investigate, while I continued with my work and kept one eye on the sloping path.

The four men were smartly dressed, with shoes as polished as their hair was slick. As they made their way down the path, I noted them looking up and around as if sizing up our farm for some grand design. One of the men carried a clipboard. The dog was doing a good job of trying to keep them in a pack, and I called him off just as soon as they saw me.

'I'll fetch him,' I told them, and headed off at a lick because I didn't feel comfortable in their presence.

When I found Father, and described the men to him, he looked back towards the farmhouse as if he'd been expecting them. Judging by the expression on his face, I was also sure that he had hoped they might not visit at all.

'The War Ag,' he muttered, before setting off to meet them. 'Let's see what they're made of, then.'

The War Agricultural Executive Committee was a government organisation set up to increase farming production during the conflict. By law, specially appointed representatives from the Committee had the authority to visit farms and dictate what crops should be grown. Early in 1940, our turn came for an inspection. Naturally, for a man who had spent his entire life farming Quarry Pits, and knew how to extract the most from every acre of the land, Father didn't take kindly to being told what to do. He greeted the men cordially, but I couldn't help noticing how he fixed each one with a penetrating gaze, as if to get the measure of this group tasked with assessing his fields. Even as a child, I could tell from the way they were dressed that these fellows weren't men of the soil. They were townies or city dwellers most probably, and that was never going to go down well with my dad.

'Do you have boots?' he asked, when they proposed a tour of the farm.

'Just lead the way,' said the man with the clipboard, as the others looked to their shoes.

I can't say whether Father deliberately took them across the soggier stretches of low-lying land, but the mud did their footwear no favours. It also brought The Sag to their attention, however. This was what we called the stretch of land where drainage was always a challenge. It was bog, basically, and good for very little but reed for thatching.

'Potatoes,' declared the fellow with the clipboard, writing out an entry at the same time. 'You'll grow a crop here.'

My father had been looking out across the stretch of land when he said this. He turned to address the man side on.

'Have you grown potatoes before?' he asked. 'It's too wet and marshy here.'

'We can't let the land go to waste,' said the man, who didn't meet his eye, though his colleagues looked very uneasy.

'The biggest waste will be our time and effort,' Father muttered under his breath, which made me smirk. This time the man with the clipboard caught my eye. He didn't look amused at all.

'Potatoes it shall be,' he repeated, and finished his entry with a tick. 'That's settled.'

As well as insisting on what crops to plant, the War Ag could also supply farms with labour when required. With so many of his men gone to fight, Father relied on a core of solid, long-serving and reliable old boys. Even so, with his workforce reduced he struggled to manage the land as well as the steam tackle. Before the committee representatives left, with shoes caked in mud, they made assistance available to my dad. Despite the clear need for more help, he seemed subdued on accepting their offer.

'No good will come from this,' he grumbled as their car could be heard pulling away. 'What I really need, Joan,' he added, as he steered me back to the farmhouse, 'is ten more helpers like you.'

It was around this time, when I was still just eight years old, that I learned to drive my first petrol-fuelled tractor. They'd been in existence for a while, but weren't commonplace across Worcestershire. When the farmer nearest to us acquired one, it was a revelation for an agricultural community that had relied on horse and steam power. I would watch from the gate as that miracle machine hauled a plough, and when the farmer asked if I'd like to get behind the wheel I jumped at the chance. Everyone knew how much I helped Father, and many recognised that I was capable of tasks beyond my age. As I often gave a helping hand to our neighbour, he was happy to let me learn. The tractor was a little orange Fordson with an open seat and rear wheels almost twice my height. I had to use both feet to depress the clutch, but once it lurched into life I soon learned to drive it as well as anyone.

'You're a wonder,' said Dad, when he first learned of my new skills. With a workforce bolstered by the War Ag, he faced a testing time. He never minded the Land Girls, who were always keen to learn, but some of the men that showed up would leave him exasperated. They all had different reasons for not fighting. Some battled illness; others had suffered injuries on the frontline. While most were willing to do their best, almost every one of them demanded a level of supervision from my dad that he couldn't afford to provide. So, the moment he discovered his second-born could drive a tractor, and plough or scuffle a field without any help at all, he ordered one for me right away.

Strictly speaking, the police might've had something to say if they'd seen a girl of my age at work behind the wheel, but this was a testing time for us all. In the countryside, we just got on with life as best we could.

When our first tractor arrived, I even unloaded it from the truck myself. Goodness knows what those volunteers made of that scene: a little one like me in charge, but I proved to them all that I could pull my weight. It was ironic, I suppose, that Father had to place a heavy anvil on the back left-hand side when ploughing. As the tractor's right-hand wheels followed the furrow that had just been ploughed, a counter ballast was needed with just me in the seat in order to maintain traction.

At school once, at harvest time for the potato crops, the children were tasked with lending a hand at a nearby farm. All we had to do was follow another new tractor as it spun up the spuds, and collect them into baskets. Our schoolmistress marshalled us there. She then handed over to a farmer, who addressed us from the footplate of his gleaming machine.

'I don't suppose any of you youngsters knows how to drive one of these?' he asked, and slapped the engine housing. 'There's other work I could be doing.'

As many of us came from farming families, one boy from my class raised his hand, as did I, but the farmer ignored me. Instead, he invited the lad to step up and try to start the thing. It wasn't easy in those days. There was no such thing as an ignition key. Instead, the boy grasped a starting handle at the front of the vehicle and began to wind it vigorously.

'You're not doing that right,' I said eventually, when the engine failed to come alive.

The farmer turned his attention to me, cupping his hand across his brow as I stood against the morning sun.

'And you can do better?' he asked.

The boy ignored me for a moment, only to fail once again in getting the engine to fire. He stood back and shook his head. Then, with some reluctance, he passed me the handle. That lad might've been bigger than me, but I was determined to show them. On the second attempt at turning the handle, with a rattle and a rumble that drew cheers from my classmates, I started her up.

For a whole week, I spun potatoes with that tractor. Unfortunately, it wasn't a task I could repeat at Quarry Pits because the crop failed miserably. As Father knew full well, that sag land was hopeless for cultivating crops. He took no pleasure in informing the War Ag that the spuds had rotted in the ground, however. My dad was as committed to the war effort as anyone, though as the conflict deepened an episode occurred one day that left me convinced it was over for us all.

Whenever the weather turned in our favour during those early war years, my brother, John, and I used to head out alone on picnics. Mother would send us off with sandwiches, which we would take across the bushy fields near the brook. This was land just off the lane that had been left to go a little wild. It was ideal for cattle grazing, until the War Ag made us dig it up. But at the time it led to a lovely ribbon of woodland where we liked to take our lunch. Brother and I were almost across the bushy fields when the sound of a large vehicle braking caught our attention.

'Who is that?' asked little John, as a military truck pulled up in the lane behind the gate.

Together, we watched a man with a rifle hop out at the passenger side of the cab, and then make his way around the vehicle. He dropped the tailgate, upon which a dozen or so figures jumped out onto the lane.

'They're soldiers,' I said, noting the uniform, though the blue circles on the back of their jackets wasn't like anything I'd seen our boys wearing. It could mean only one thing, I thought with a gasp as John reached up and found my hand. 'The Germans have landed!'

With our worst fears apparently taking shape in front of us, Brother and I turned tail and ran for our lives. We were close to the woodlands, and instinctively that seemed like the safest place to hide.

'Don't let them get us!' cried John as we hurtled under the tree canopy.

'Stay quiet!' I dropped down into the bracken just inside the woods, and scrambled to the edge so I could observe.

By then, the soldiers were making their way diagonally across the bushy fields, heading for the brook. The man from the cab, along with the driver, walked alongside them. Both were clutching rifles across their chest.

Without doubt, I decided, barely able to muster a breath, the invasion that everyone feared had begun.

With little John at my side, pale and frightened just like me, we kept our heads low and hoped the Nazis would not see us. Lying in the undergrowth, facing each other, I promised Brother that I would take good care of him if we were captured. Eventually, after half an hour or so, I braved looking up again. The truck was still parked on the lane, and I could hear voices down by the brook. They most definitely weren't speaking English.

'I'm hungry,' said Brother in a whisper. 'I'm hungry and I'd like to go home.'

'We can't risk moving,' I told him. 'They'll see us as soon as we cross the field.'

John seemed most upset at this, so I decided that perhaps we'd

47

both feel better if we ate our sandwiches. We did so carefully, trying hard not to make a sound, and then settled down once more. After several hours, with those voices still audible from the brook, we hatched an escape plan. It was John who spotted the puffballs sprouting from a rotted trunk near our hiding place. He crawled out to break off the fungus, and then returned to show that crushing the heads produced a nutty brown powder in the palm of his hand.

'Look,' he said, and daubed a stripe on his wrist. 'They'll never see us with this.'

By now, I was ready to act on any suggestion. Quickly we crushed up the puffballs and then painted our hands and faces. I'm not quite sure how we thought this would disguise us against the Nazis in broad daylight, but it steeled us to crawl from our hiding places and prepare to make a break for it.

Just as we did so, however, the voices from the brook became clearer and more forceful. I looked down the field and saw a line of men climb up from the bank. Our timing couldn't have been worse. All we could do was retreat into the woods once more and wait for them to drive away. We were still so frightened that we didn't dare leave for some time after the truck had followed the lane over the fold. When we did brave venturing into the open, brother John and I ran all the way back to the farmhouse without stopping.

'Where have you been?' asked Mother when we tore through the door, though her concern turned to puzzlement on seeing our camouflaged faces.

Breathlessly, as Dad arrived to see what the commotion was all about, I reported our Nazi encounter, from the truck to the guns and the striking blue circles on the back of their jackets.

'And you saw this down by the brook?' he said, as if reading my mind.

John nodded, wiping his cheeks with the heel of his hand. We had been hiding for hours, and the build-up of tension had finally got the better of him.

'What will happen now?' he asked.

Father considered this for a moment, glanced at Mum, and smiled.

'Well, I dare say the water down there will be running a little more freely,' he declared with a grin. 'Children, they were prisoners of war! Those blue circles mean they're Italian, I believe.'

'There's a new camp near here,' Mother added. 'Those men have been put to work.'

I felt a great weight leave my shoulders on hearing this, but after such a frightening experience it didn't stop my brother and I from sobbing. It was the first time we had encountered enemy soldiers, even if they had been here as prisoners of war, but it also wasn't the last. Within the year, one became such a familiar face at Quarry Pits that we would consider him part of the family.

8

The Trusted

German POWs, Bruno and Karl. Karl became a dear friend.

He didn't say much at all on his arrival. The escorting officer introduced him to Father as Karl. The man shook my dad's hand, but only briefly raised his gaze. Watching from the kitchen with Mother and my siblings, I was simply struck by how humbled he appeared.

'You're welcome to work for me,' said Father, speaking up as if the fellow were deaf and not German. 'Just as long as you cause me no trouble.'

I'm not sure the poor chap understood fully, in view of his grasp of the language at the time, but Karl nodded, keeping his gaze on the floor still.

'I never wanted to fight,' he said quietly, in laboured English, as if it were something he had practised so that his intentions would be quite clear.

The POW camps near us had filled up fast. Many of the inmates were put to work under supervision, like the Italians we had encountered. After that day in the bushy fields, we began to see such details of men all around the countryside. Eventually, the military took the decision to select the most trustworthy and compliant prisoners, and offer them individually as unguarded labour.

A German conscript, Karl had been captured early during the war. After some time inside his camp, he'd proven himself to be one of the *Trusteds* – a compliant prisoner who could work without military supervision during the day. It was the War Ag who assigned Karl to Quarry Pits, and that proved to be one of the most helpful things they ever did for us. The man was a blacksmith by trade, and Father was in dire need of such a skilled hand to maintain his steam tackle.

Karl had a long face, both physically and in spirit, with a receding hairline that he swept back to the nape of his neck. Despite being so clearly occupied by his thoughts, he quickly proved himself to be a dedicated worker. Father was very impressed. Often, when the guards arrived to collect Karl at the end of each day, my dad would remark on his diligence and the quality of his craft.

Over the course of that year, Karl spent most of his time in the workshop at Quarry Pits. Inside the hot, dimly lit space, he would forge, hammer, cut, bend and buckle all manner of iron and steel parts for the engines and the implements. From time to time, if things didn't meet his exacting standards, he would reveal himself to have quite a temper. You always knew when something hadn't worked out on account of all the cursing in his mother tongue, accompanied by the clatter of tools as he flung them into the courtyard. Dad didn't mind so much. He said it was the sign of someone who took great pride in his work. Karl was certainly dedicated; with his shirtsleeves rolled to the elbow, or just a vest tucked into his trousers when the temperature climbed, he would break only for a smoke or a bite to eat in the yard, and that's when we talked.

Our conversations were broken to begin with. I spoke no German, but Karl made every effort with us. Slowly, as our trust in him grew, he found his voice in English. I was no more than ten or eleven at the time, while Karl was in his mid-thirties. Even so, we found a certain level on which to communicate that was based on honesty rather than age. During those chats, I learned how grateful he was to Father for this opportunity, and the chance to feel that he was making good use of his skills. And while he didn't like to talk about his time at the frontline, which seemed to strike him as a source of shame, he spoke openly about the one aspect of his former life that he missed more than anything else.

'My sweetheart,' he would say, having learned the word from a German-to-English dictionary I gave him as a gift.

A private man in many respects, Karl never shared much about the girl he had left behind, but it was evident to us all that she meant the world to him. When he did mention her, that long face would light up with a smile that offered some glimpse of what he'd looked like before the war changed the course of his life.

After a year at Quarry Pits, escorted to and from work by prison truck each day, Karl was permitted to move in with us on a permanent basis. This was regarded as a great privilege, not just by the army but by Karl himself. He took up residence in one of the wagons the men used to sleep in when the ploughing engines were contracted out. Father kept it across from the cherry orchard away to the east of the farmhouse. It was cosy – oval topped with a varnished wood interior, a bunk, stove and little kitchen – and Karl made it his own. There, he would compose plaintive letters home, and place his faith in the Red Cross postal system to ensure safe passage.

Some months after he moved in with us, Karl began to receive letters at the farm. They had been sent to the camp, and were delivered by the military police who sometimes dropped in unannounced to check on him. The letters had already been opened and censored. Yet even with so many black lines crossed through each hand-written note, they would have a profound effect on the German.

'She's replied,' Dad would say whenever Karl hurried away to read them. 'Best give him some space.'

I followed Dad's advice, of course, but when Karl did emerge from his workshop or the wagon, the red rims around his eyes told us all how much he missed her. Sometimes, with his composure restored, he would talk of his happiness and relief to learn that she was well and in good spirits.

'We'll be together again one day,' he assured me with some confidence. 'Until then, there's work to be done!'

As a blacksmith, Karl was considered invaluable by Father. By now, several years into his stay on the farm, he was as trusted as any other farm-hand. It was easy to forget that he was here as a wartime prisoner. On one occasion, that came close to costing us all very dearly indeed.

'It's always the rooks,' muttered Father, narrowing his gaze.

Minutes earlier, I had accompanied him out to Karl's wagon so he could go over the latest inventory of repairs. As soon as the wagon came into view, where Karl was washing dishes outside, our presence had caused a flock of birds to take wing from the cherry orchard.

Just then both men were inspecting what was left of the fruit I held out in my hand. I had picked them out of the long grass under the boughs of the trees. Karl took one look at the pecked flesh and confirmed Father's suspicions.

'They feast here all the time,' he said, and gestured at the wagon. 'I suppose they've just grown used to me.'

'I'll have to come back and wait.' Father slipped his cap from his head and rested his hands on his waist. 'The twelve-bore will be sure to scare them off.'

My dad kept the shotgun inside the farmhouse, which he used on the birds when they became a nuisance.

'I can take care of that,' said Karl, quite casually, without taking his eyes off the orchard. 'If you'll permit me,' he added, before facing around.

I watched my father meet his gaze. After what felt like an age,

Dad nodded as if satisfied by a question he had just answered for himself.

'If you can save what's left of the crop, Karl,' he said eventually. 'I'll be grateful to you.'

And that's how our guest, a German prisoner of war, came to take possession of the weapon. That evening, at supper, we heard shots crackle over the fields. We were having supper at the time. I glanced at Father, as did Marian, little John and our mum, but he made no remark and just carried on eating. The next morning, we found Karl had proven himself to have quite an aim. The rooks were nowhere to be seen, having taken flight, he told us, just as soon as he opened fire on them. My father nodded, assessing the cherry orchard and the coal-black feathers on the ground, and suggested that Karl hold on to the shotgun.

'If they come back,' he said, 'let them have it.'

His decision to allow Karl to keep the gun seemed quite sensible to me. Not once had he given us any cause for concern. Sure enough, he kept a watchful eye on that orchard, and the cherry harvest turned out to be particularly fruitful that year. I forgot all about the weapon, in fact, and I imagine Father did, too. Until, one morning at breakfast, Mother answered a knock at the farmhouse door to find the military police had come to stage a spot inspection.

'Everything is fine,' said Father, stepping in just as soon as they had declared their intentions. 'Karl is one of us.'

'Well, that's good to hear,' said the officer in charge. 'But perhaps you'll allow us to draw that conclusion for ourselves.'

Of course, my thoughts turned to the twelve-bore, and I'm sure the very same thing went through my dad's mind.

'You'll find Karl in the workshop,' he told them, which was true as we'd already said hello to him that morning. 'He likes to fire up the forge to make the most of the day.'

'Then perhaps you'll take us to him,' said the officer. The two men who accompanied him both carried rifles. I avoided their eyes and hoped I wouldn't faint from fright.

'I'll show you the way.' Father invited them to step outside, and held the door for the officer before following on from behind. As he did so, he glanced over his shoulder and caught my eye.

I knew just what I had to do.

Mother was well aware of our predicament. Like everyone in the family, she had grown very fond of our quiet, hardworking and lovelorn blacksmith. She made me wait for a minute, until she could be sure that Father and the soldiers had reached the workshop, and then sent me on my way like a rabbit out of a trap. I didn't stop for breath, hurtling up the path with my eyes fixed on the wagon just as soon as it became visible. Inside, with my heart hammering, I found the gun propped at the foot of his bed. I grabbed it without further thought, and then froze. It hadn't occurred to me where I might hide the weapon, and so I simply scrambled from the wagon and ran for covered ground. I stayed out of sight, in shock but sure that we had done the right thing. Minutes later, I watched Father and Karl accompany the inspection team to the wagon. It was a day I'll never forget, and though my dad and Karl were quick to chuckle afterwards – and praise my good work – they were both as shaken as me.

Karl stayed at Quarry Pits for almost seven years. Like every prisoner of war, he shared our relief when the conflict came to an end, and looked forward to the day when he'd finally be permitted to rebuild his life back home. It took a long time before the military authorised the prisoners' repatriation. When that day arrived, Karl greeted it with mixed emotions. Here was someone set to reunite with his one true love, and yet he had settled with us. Farming at Quarry Pits had become his way of life. The man had set down roots, made the workshop his own, and now he had to leave.

We didn't hear from Karl for quite some time. When the letter arrived, however, his news came as quite a shock. For he had made it back home and immediately sought out his sweetheart, only to discover that she had been less than honest with him through the war years. Perhaps it was the sheer force of affection in his correspondence that had prevented her from telling the truth, or maybe she withheld it for the sake of keeping his spirits up, but the fact was she had met someone else soon after Karl's capture, and had two children by him.

We lost contact with our German friend in the years that followed. In his final letters, Karl expressed a desire to return to Quarry Pits that bordered on desperation, but the authorities just didn't permit it at that time. I believe he went on to play an important role in civic life, and even served as mayor in his community. I just hope that he found happiness, because Karl was a good man and I will always be grateful that he came into our lives despite the circumstances.

9
Home Guard

John and I with the men clearing scrub.

It was a blessing to have Karl working with us. Farming can be a tough business at the best of times, and throughout those years his commitment was greatly appreciated. Father showed the same sense of gratitude to all his men when the younger ones left for the frontline. They might've been getting on, but compared to the volunteers from the War Ag this loyal band put their heart and soul into the work.

Among others, there was Harry Taylor, Arthur Wilkins, Tom Roberts, Frank Davis and Bill Allen. They all got along famously with Father, and despite the creaking limbs and sore backs at the end of each long day, none of them seriously complained about the extra demands placed upon them. If anything, they took up the challenge with vigour. And together with my brother, John, we'd do our best to support them.

Our main task in taking care of these old boys, and keeping their spirits up, was to provide them with a steady supply of hot coffee.

If we weren't helping out in the fields, Brother and I would be standing in front of the Aga in the kitchen waiting for the kettle to boil. The men liked their hot drinks with plenty of sugar. They needed the energy, I suppose.

Of course, we were on rations back then, and needed to be careful. With our own cattle, some provisions like milk and cream were never in short supply, but other essentials would often run dry. One time, having promised the men a nice hot cup of coffee, Brother and I found the jar was all but empty.

'What shall we do?' I asked, and showed John the jar. With the kettle on, and the men working up a thirst, it seemed like such a shame. Even the tea leaves were in short supply, I discovered, which is when John hit upon a plan.

'Trust me,' he said, and promptly slid a chair across to the dresser.

As soon as I saw that determined look upon his face, I knew that whatever my brother had in mind he'd see it through to the end. He clambered up onto the chair and reached for a tin on one of the upper shelves.

'Stock cubes?' I said, and laughed despite myself as he climbed back down with the tin. 'We're supposed to be making coffee, not preparing Sunday Roast!'

John pushed the chair to one side, and shot me a mischievous grin.

'Well, it will be the same colour as coffee,' he said, before removing the lid from the tin. Peeling a cube and holding it to his nostrils, Brother took a sniff and then pulled a face. 'It'll be fine with milk,' he said, just as the kettle came to the boil. 'Lucky we have plenty of that.'

'John, they've been drinking coffee since long before we were born!' I said. 'If it doesn't taste right, they'll know!'

Brother switched his attention to the kettle, which was whistling merrily on the stove, and then returned his gaze to me.

'Are you going to face them empty-handed?' he asked.

Normally, when it was time for coffee, the men would break off from their work and gather outside Karl's workshop. Sure enough, that's where John and I found them when we took the tray out from the farmhouse. They were chatting and laughing about some story Arthur Wilkins was spinning. He could always keep them entertained on a break. Approaching them with our hot and thoroughly savoury drinks, I just hoped the tale he was telling would keep them so occupied they wouldn't register anything else.

'There you are, Joan!' declared Arthur, having delivered what sounded like a punch-line to much mirth from the others. I watched his eyes fall upon the steaming cups crammed onto the tray, and wished I had overruled my brother. It didn't help matters that John had suddenly chosen to trail some way behind me. I was on my own. There was no turning back. All I could do was set the tray down on a crate and then step back smartly so the men could gather round. Arthur collected his drink, grasping it with both hands. Then, with his eyes closed, he held it up to inhale the aroma.

'Hello? What do we have here then?'

With my breath bated, I watched him open his eyes and look directly at me.

Minutes earlier, back in the kitchen, with eddies still turning in the cups of brown liquid that we had stirred, John looked as wary as me.

'It smells of stock cube,' he said, though I didn't need to be told.

'Brother, it *reeks* of stock cube!' I waited for him to look at me. 'What are we going to do?'

John considered this for a moment, looking very serious indeed. Then an idea must've popped into his head because delight sprang into his expression.

'Sugar!' he said, and rushed to fetch the bag. 'They all take a lot of sugar. We just need to give them a little more!'

Frank and Harry Taylor would often take three teaspoons, while the others would settle for two. Watching my brother heap four, five and then six into each cup, I asked out loud whether he had gone barmy.

'What's Mother going to say for one thing?' I questioned, and took the bag from him. 'That's a day's worth of sugar gone to waste!'

'But it isn't a waste,' said John, and stirred each cup once more.

This time, he dared to take a sip from one. I watched him smack his lips while trying hard not to grimace.

'Tastes good,' he said, and set the cup back on the tray.

'Like a stock cube?' I asked, to clarify.

Brother stood back so I could take the tray.

'Sweeter,' he said, with some pride, like he'd just invented a winning formula.

Facing Dad's men out in the courtyard, I didn't feel so confident. Arthur Wilkins had just taken a swig and appeared to be assessing the taste with his gaze fixed on me.

'Well,' he declared after a moment, addressing the others as much as me. 'That hits the spot!'

I breathed out in relief so forcefully that I swear Dad noticed. All I could do as they struck up in conversation once more was retreat to where my brother was watching and then turn tail before we burst out laughing.

'Didn't I tell you everything would work out fine,' said John, when we were safely out of earshot. 'You just have to trust me, Joan. I'll look out for you.'

'We look out for each other,' I said, and declined his suggestion that we make some more for ourselves.

Brother John was by my side, in fact, on the night the northeast horizon lit up like a forge.

The bombing runs had become a regular feature of our lives by then. I still went around the outside of the house at dusk each day, helping Mother and Marian to secure the curtains, but by then the eerie drone that would later cut through the darkness no longer sent me scuttling. On that night, midway through November, we had heard the planes in the distance and the dull thuds that followed. On this occasion, however, those thuds had been so numerous it felt like it might never end. We both knew that it was Coventry. The Luftwaffe had been targeting the city for months, but never like this.

'Those poor sods,' Dad said, when he came out to fetch us in. Standing behind my brother and me, he placed a hand on each of our shoulders and just watched as that awful band flickered and flexed under the caul of the night.

'Should we sleep in the cellar?' asked John, who had watched in silent awe.

I sensed Father squeeze my shoulder, and imagine he did the same with his son.

'There's no need,' he said with some confidence. 'We're quite safe inside.'

Like every household across the country, we had taken steps to create a place of refuge during raids. While many families took to Anderson shelters in their gardens, or huddled under dining-room tables, our farmhouse had a subterranean space that was as secure as any fortress. Apart from John and I, the family had to hunch low at the foot of the steps to clear the vaulted brick ceiling. Mother stocked it with provisions, but we never once spent time down there – at least not as a precaution during the bombing raids – and this was down to another of Dad's passions in life.

When Father wasn't cultivating the land or tending to his cattle, he'd always be found under the farmhouse. There in that cool cellar space, illuminated by the single natural light well or working by gas lamps whenever the sun went down, my dad devoted himself to cider-making.

With a mill and a press, hand-built with wood and iron, as well as pails, buckets and flagons, there was often little room to move. It was a pastime Father took very seriously, however, as did the men who worked for him. In particular, the older generation brought their wisdom and experience to the craft. In fact, they would often be found down there working alongside my dad with the same dedication that they showed in the fields.

Unlike the coffee, the cider they made was a form of refreshment that could never be substituted. Like Father, Harry Taylor, Arthur Wilkins, Tom, Frank and Bill were connoisseurs. They would always carry a flagon with them, out into the fields, claiming it quenched their thirst when the sun beat down upon them. One advantage of age, I suppose, was the fact that the men were sensible about their drink. They all had jobs to do, and with the younger generation absent they carried them out to the best of their abilities.

As well as his work on the farm, Harry Taylor served in the Home Guard. In his mid-sixties, he often talked about his rank and the importance of his role. Dad and the other men would have listened to him as they worked, but I can't say they paid much attention. It was just something that made Harry feel good about himself, and so nobody took him to task. Whenever he made a song and dance about some classified military operation he was set to undertake, someone would always shoot me a look and roll their eyes. If it was that crucial to the war effort, I thought to myself, why was he telling everyone about it?

At the end of each day, the men would set off for their homes, on foot or by bicycle, and leave Father and I to catch up with Karl. We'd find him in the workshop, dealing with an endless stream of repairs. Father kept a tight rein on the maintenance of his steam tackle, but sometimes an emergency call would come from a farm that had contracted out his equipment, and he'd be required on site at a moment's notice to deal with a breakdown. One evening, he was called out to replace a part on one of the threshing machines, and I went with him. During the war, travelling by car at night was a challenge. To avoid being seen from the air Dad drove with headlamps masked by sackcloth. Frankly, it was easier to navigate by moonlight, but we reached the farm eventually.

The machine had been left for him in the Dutch barn. The floor was littered with straw, though much of it had been swept up against the bales to one side. There was nobody about, and with the farmhouse some distance from the barn my dad just decided we should get on with the job. While I held our lamp so he could see, Father got underneath the thresher to work on what proved to be an awkward and frustrating job. My arm was beginning to ache when he finally made some progress.

'We'll be heading home shortly,' he said, catching my eye from underneath the machine.

'Good,' I said. 'It's getting late and Mother will be worried.'

She was always wary when we left the house after dark, and visibly relieved on our return. Ever since war broke out, talk of an invasion never went away. Like dealing with the threat of a fox around the hen houses, we couldn't afford to drop our guard.

'I'd sooner deal with your mother,' joked Dad, 'than face an angry farmer in the morning because the tackle is out of action.'

I chuckled, as did he, and that's when we heard voices approaching.

'Who is that?' I asked in a whisper.

'Douse the light!' Already, Dad was bolt upright. Hearing footsteps accompanying the voices, I did as he was told and extinguished the lamp's flame.

Immediately, we were left with only the light from the moon. It was a clear night, and beams slanted through gaps in the barn timbers.

'The Germans?' I asked under my breath, to which Dad responded by grabbing my wrist and breaking into a dash across the barn. By now, we could see lamp lights rocking through the darkness accompanied by the sound of boots on the earth. With my heart kicking like a mule, my imagination took over. All I could do was follow Dad into the straw pile and help him drag it over us so we were hidden from sight.

'Not a word!' he hissed, and froze like me as the lamplight strengthened.

From our hiding place, with wide eyes and fearful, I watched a band of figures stop at the entrance. They were soldiers, armed with rifles, but in silhouette with the moon behind them I couldn't be sure what side they were on.

A minute later, having walked full circle around the engine, and even prodded at the straw nearby with his bayonet, the soldier in charge sounded the all-clear.

'Must've been vermin,' I heard him say in plain English, much to my relief, though I didn't dare breathe out in case I was mistaken.

Even my dad waited until their voices began to trail away. Only when we were sure that they were long gone did we emerge, brush the straw from our clothes and chuckle at the turn of events. Those soldiers might've been on our side, but they'd hardly proven themselves to be the finest of patrols.

Mother didn't find our story amusing, of course. She was just thankful that we had made it back in one piece. We could've been run through, she said the next morning. A case of mistaken identity with fatal consequences. Dad just nodded like she had a point, before holding open the kitchen door for me as I had the coffee tray in my hands. The old boys had gathered in the courtyard, which they often did to await instructions for the day. As they each took a cup from the tray in turn, I was able to look them in the eye with nothing to hide this time. Then I reached Harry Taylor, who continued with a conversation as he collected his coffee, and his words caused me to freeze on the spot.

'... so, as soon as we heard activity in the barn, we investigated,' he said. 'I swear someone had been in there, but whoever it was must've taken one look at my patrol and run for the hills. Oh, yes,' he said, and took his first swig of coffee. 'If it was the enemy then they were wise not to tangle with the likes of me.'

Just then, I caught Dad's eye. He shot me a wink, before commending Harry for his service to the crown.

'Men like you are the reason my family can sleep safely in their beds at night,' he said. ''Ain't that right, Joan?'

'Yes, Sir,' I agreed, with my eyes fixed on the tray and my cheeks burning brightly.

10

The Elephant that Came to Stay

Riding my horse Sparks with our dog Mick.

Like any rural household during the war, we took in our share of evacuees. While many families sheltered children from the towns and cities, we were allocated adults. Three couples took up residence with us in turn. They were retired folk who had been bombed out of their homes in Birmingham. It was a difficult time for everyone, but I couldn't help feeling disappointed when they arrived. Mother always put on a big welcome for them. She'd have tea and cakes ready, and show them around the farmhouse, but it was never fully appreciated. Having grown up at Quarry Pits, this was my first real encounter with townies. I didn't like them much.

For one thing, Marian and I had to give up our bedroom for them. We were put in with our Auntie Maud, who was also living with us at the time. We didn't mind, but the evacuees showed no gratitude. One old couple, Mr and Mrs Aston, spent most of their time shut away from us, in fact. She would knit or play cards while he just read the newspaper. John, Marian and I often took them cups of tea, and they'd respond like we were house servants.

'They didn't travel far to get here,' grumbled Dad one time, who steered clear of them as much as possible. 'Yet they might as well have come from another world.'

Mother was always quick to point out that these people had lost their homes. Even so, they tested her patience on many occasions. For one thing, she cooked all their meals, and none of them once offered to help. Instead, I'd run upstairs to announce that supper was served, and they'd file out with poker faces as if perhaps they had been expecting it half an hour earlier.

The evacuees would always eat separately from us. I didn't mind. Whenever they were seated in the dining room, a stiff and uneasy atmosphere would set in. I felt as though I would have to be on my best behaviour, while Mother and Marian complained that it seemed like nothing was ever good enough for them. The food was a case in point. Mother was a creative cook who took great pride in feeding her family. She made the most of whatever was in season, and let nothing go to waste.

Unfortunately, couples like Mr and Mrs Aston failed to truly appreciate her efforts.

'This meat,' Mr Aston once said to me, having called me back from serving their suppers. He poked at his food with his fork. 'What is it?'

Mother had cooked a lovely rabbit stew. It really was a mouth-watering meal. Rich and perfectly seasoned, she had cooked it in a stock with cider, carrots and streaky bacon. With a plentiful supply of rabbits in the wild at Quarry Pits, my mum considered it to be as cheap as it was nourishing. By then I was old enough to appreciate good cooking, and happily cleared my plate.

Facing Mr Aston across the table, while his wife picked at her food as if it might have broken glass in it, I told him what I had just served.

'Rabbit?' he said, repeating what I had said with a note of disgust.

In response, Mrs Aston issued a sound like a field mouse expiring and set down her knife and fork. I glanced at her plate. She had barely touched her food.

'It's very good,' I assured them, standing with one hand clasping my wrist. 'I'm sure you'll develop a taste for it.'

'I appreciate the efforts your mother has made.' Mr Aston dabbed his mouth with his serviette. 'But there are limits, girl.'

I left the dining room carrying their plates as well as a sense of anger and indignation. As soon as I arrived in the kitchen, where Marian was washing up pots, she saw the untouched food and read my expression straight away.

'Is nothing good enough for them?' she asked.

'They could at least help with the dishes,' I grumbled. 'Though I'm beginning to wonder why we bother feeding them at all.'

Mother had just been finishing her rounds in the incubator room. She emerged to see me scraping the Astons' plates into the dog bowl.

'At least it's not going to waste,' she said, having paused in her tracks for a moment and sighed to herself. 'To be frank, I'm running out of recipes they might like.'

I took the bowl to the kitchen door. Outside, the dog was waiting hungrily to be fed. I had trained him to sit for his supper, and wait for my signal before he could begin.

'There's nothing wrong with rabbit,' I said, and closed the door on the sound of hungry chomping. I looked Mother in the eye, and then smiled to myself on hatching a plan. 'Maybe the secret is in how you present it.'

The next time Mother cooked with rabbit, a casserole with rosemary and fresh potatoes, she called me in to serve our guests. Before I did so, however, I set the plates on the side and set about carving the jointed pieces of meat.

'What difference will that make?' asked Mother. 'The Astons know what they don't like, and rabbit is at the top of their list.'

'It isn't rabbit,' I said, concentrating as I positioned my fork into a section of saddle and began to cut it into slices.

Finally, with my work complete, I carried the dishes through to the dining room. John had run upstairs to let the Astons know that supper was served. I found them both settling into their seats. I can only imagine that the aroma from the kitchen must've met them in the hall, because they looked warily at each other before turning their attention to me.

'Mother has cooked this especially for you.' With relish, I set their plates in front of them. Mr and Mrs Aston appraised the stew looking most unimpressed. 'It's a casserole,' I said, and took a step back towards the door. *Chicken* casserole.'

Mr Aston bowed his head as if he was about to say grace, and then looked up at me with a smile.

'My favourite,' he said. 'You're spoiling us.'

I was giggling before I closed the dining-room door behind me. Together with John, I hurried back to the kitchen where Mother made me confess what I had done. She looked unimpressed, until Marian burst out laughing, and then she couldn't resist cracking a smile.

'Wait until your father finds out,' she warned me, trying hard to sound serious, but I wasn't worried. If anything, I decided, it would make his day.

I should say my high spirits turned to trepidation when I dared to return to the dining room. I entered cautiously to find both Mr and Mrs Aston sitting there with empty plates and an air of satisfaction.

'Please do pass on our compliments to the chef,' said Mr Aston, as I cleared away the table.

'That was the most remarkable chicken we've ever tasted,' his wife added, and offered me a smile for the first time since they had moved in with us.

'We'll be sure to serve it again,' I told them, ignoring the stifled laughter I could hear from the hall.

Disguising the food was one thing, but there was nothing we could do to make our surroundings more appetising to our guests. Through my eyes, I couldn't think of a better place to live. From dawn until dusk, there was always work to be done on the farm. It was often hard but always rewarding, and yet the evacuees just refused to be involved.

Sometimes they would leave the door to their room ajar. I would pass by and see them sitting there in a silence broken only by the ticking of the clock. They even seemed oblivious to the sunshine streaming in from outside. The sight left me feeling strangely sad, and all the more convinced that I never wanted to live in a town or a city. For it seemed such a waste to be missing out, shut off from life like that, but clearly they were set in their ways.

While growing up, I spent more time outside than I did in the farmhouse, come rain or shine. My home reached across one hundred acres, and I was familiar with every sight and sound.

So, when a strange and protracted blast rose into the air one sunny day, as though a trumpet player had just tootled on his instrument, I remarked upon it straight away.

'What is that?' I asked one of the men working alongside me.

With his hand supporting the small of his back, Arthur Wilkins stood tall and listened keenly. A moment later, the same sound cut through the breeze and birdsong once again.

'I must be mistaken,' he said, his eyes narrowing. 'But one thing is for sure, it's coming from the lane.'

We weren't alone in investigating. By the time we crossed the fields to the yard, farm-hands from across Quarry Pits had been drawn by the noise.

'Should I fetch the shotgun?' asked John, as we followed Father up the track towards the farm gate.

Dad glanced over his shoulder, frowning at the same time. I told my little brother to stay close to me, just in case.

What we found parked in front of the farm gate took my breath away. It wasn't the sight of a steam lorry with the driver and his mate looking downcast on the verge that did it. It was the load on the trailer: a huge cage that housed an elephant.

'I've seen them in books,' I told John as the leathery giant eyed us all and swished its great ears. The sight made me laugh out loud, while the men gathered round and declared that they never believed they would see such a thing. An elephant in Inkberrow, here in the heart of Worcestershire.

'Is it real?' asked John, who had yet to blink. 'Does it bite?'

'She's a gentle soul,' answered the driver of the lorry, who had just explained to my father that one of the trailer wheel bearings was broken. 'Just hot and very thirsty.'

They were circus hands, we learned, stranded here with no way of alerting the convoy and the elephant's keeper who were travelling ahead.

'We can't have that,' said Father with a grin. 'She is welcome to stay with us while we get you roadworthy once more. And if she can pull a plough then she'll pay her way.'

It took a moment for the circus hands to realise my dad wasn't being entirely serious, much to the amusement of his men. By now, even Mother and Marian had ventured out to see what was going on. Mum stopped dead in her tracks, while Marian simply looked on in disbelief as the elephant was led down the ramp and across to its temporary new quarters at Quarry Pits.

The barn was never designed for an animal of this size, but it housed her just beautifully. The circus hand staked the ground and secured her to a long chain, which allowed her to move around. The elephant had only come into my life an hour earlier, but already I was smitten.

'What a magnificent creature,' I said, gathered with the men as we watched her feeding on fodder that the driver had on board the truck, as well as all the fruit that we could find. With a water trough for her to drink from, which we had to keep filling, my brother and I spent the rest of that day in the company of that extraordinary animal. Dad and his men managed to repair the wheel bearing, but when it came to returning the elephant to the trailer she wouldn't budge.

'She must think this is a holiday,' said the driver of the truck, having given up trying to coax her out.

There was only one thing for it. The keeper would have to be fetched. One of the farm-hands had a motorbike. He roared off with coordinates on a map that wouldn't see him return until the next day, with a passenger riding pillion. I made the most of the time it gave us in the company of the best house guest we'd ever had. We were told to keep a safe distance on account of her huge size, but it was clear that we were in the presence of a sweet and playful soul. All we had to do was meet her gaze to register that she knew we were doing our best for her. I barely slept while she was with us, and nor did John. It was all just too exciting.

In the presence of the keeper, a nice old boy who couldn't stop apologising and thanking us for our time, the elephant moved without resistance. She seemed so happy to be with him, and he was clearly grateful for the care we had shown her. John and I helped to escort our new friend from the farm with tears coursing down our cheeks. She was such a lovely thing, so clearly capable of having fun; on lumbering back up the slope with us, she reached up with her trunk and twanged an overhanging branch. It was an episode that we would never forget. One of many that shaped our lives at Quarry Pits.

I sometimes wonder what memories the Astons took with them when they finally packed their bags. On a farm that hosted so many magical moments, no doubt they would've been richer for the experience had they just stepped outside – even briefly – and simply opened their eyes.

II

Two Fronts

Loading hay with John and David Hughes.

Despite the looming threat, the German invasion never came. Instead, throughout those wartime years, we suffered another occupation at Quarry Pits. It arrived on two fronts, and I faced up to them both.

After ploughing and scuffling the soil in autumn, and planting through to spring, we always used to hold out hope for a glorious summer and fields of swaying corn. Unfortunately, however, the season didn't always shine brightly upon us. If it rained with no sign of a let-up, Father would be faced with the risk of a spoiled crop. Sometimes, the only option was to harvest and let it finish drying under shelter, which we did by creating ricks.

Having cut the crop at the stalk, we'd band it into bundles and then pack each one in layers on raised platforms. Our ricks were huge. They could finish up to thirty feet high and double the size in length. A thatcher would then climb up to weave a roof over the top in order to protect it from the elements. In time, these huge stacks would dry out, but we had to keep a watchful eye. If a rick contained a great deal of moisture, the heart of it could heat up and even combust. As a precaution, Father would often ask me to run a long metal rod into the middle of the stack on a regular basis to check the temperature. After half an hour I would pull the rod out and if it was too hot to handle we could be in trouble.

Thankfully for us the rod never got too hot but on other farms some were not so lucky. In many cases when the rick has got too hot in the middle, people have tried to save it by opening it up, with terrible consequences. Air is allowed to reach the heated core and ignition takes place. An inferno ensues, and with the danger of fire spreading to other ricks, all could be lost.

Threshing those ricks started in late autumn or early winter, and under Father's guidance, the barn would eventually be filled with dry straw bales and granary sacks of wheat or barley no matter what weather we'd had. First, however, we had to put every bundle from the rick through the threshing machine to separate the straw and the grain from the chaff, and that's when the first band of intruders came to light. It meant that, as well as threshing being demanding work, we'd have to be ready for battle.

'They're in there,' said Father one time, once he'd assessed the rick we were due to thresh. 'They won't come out until they're desperate, but when they do,' he added, 'they'll attack the smallest among us.'

With hot drinks handed out, I had joined my dad and his crew as they assembled in the rick yard ready for the day. The earliest to arrive had already lit the firebox inside the traction engine to power the threshing machine. Even at rest, with the pistons still, the firebox could sound like a beast exhaling. A dawn chill gripped the air, but with a clear sky, the heat and smoke from the engine, and a hard day's labour ahead, some of the farm-hands had already rolled up their sleeves in anticipation. Two Land Army girls had also joined us that day. Kath and Brinie were only young women, but since I was half their height all attention turned to me.

'Joan can cut the bands,' Harry Taylor suggested, while addressing my father, and then gestured towards the top of the threshing machine. 'They won't get her up there.'

'They won't get me down here either,' declared Brinie, and braced a pitchfork as if to defend herself. 'I'm ready.'

Her fellow Land Girl, Kath, looked uneasily at her.

'Maybe someone else would prefer to take my place,' I offered. 'I don't mind.'

'We're here to do a job,' said Kath, a little hesitantly perhaps, but it earned a nod of approval from her friend.

'Joan,' said Dad, and jabbed a thumb towards the contraption geared to swallow the sheaves and disgorge the corn. 'Get up there.'

I did as I was told, and not unhappily because it was an important job. Once that thresher was up and running, with its moving belts and drums, everyone had to focus on making sure the work ran smoothly.

'Don't worry,' my dad assured the Land Girls with a wink. 'If they come at you just scream.'

'Rest assured we'll do just that,' said Kath, who was smiling now.

'Me too,' said Harry, grinning broadly. 'I hate rats.'

We had dogs with us that day. They played an essential role in the threshing process. For in drying out, that rick had come to provide the perfect habitat for the worst kind of vermin. It was warm and offered a plentiful supply of food. As soon as we set to work, it wouldn't take long before one or two would break from their hiding place. As it had been wet that year, and he had seen a few around, Father decided to lay wire fencing around the yard perimeter to stop them from escaping. It meant the moment a rat scuttled into the open, the dogs would be upon them. And in the seconds before they did so, having scuttled across her feet, young Kath filled her lungs and shrieked.

'Make them stop!' she wailed, and flinched as another rat darted across the floor. With the dogs barking and the men laughing, it was quite a scene for me to take in from my perch on top of the machine. 'Please, Mr Collins. I don't like this one bit.'

My dad liked his fun, but he never took things too far, and elected to work close by the two Land Girls.

He also knew that as the rick began to shrink in size, things were set to get much worse.

'Most of them will have taken refuge at the bottom,' he said, hefting a bundle from the stack. 'When there's nowhere left for them to hide,' he added, 'they will attack.'

Poor Kath looked set to faint at this. I offered to take her place again, but she seemed to gather her wits at this and declined my kind offer.

'I'm not scared,' she said, despite her ghostly pallor. 'We want to do our bit.'

'You're made of strong stuff,' said Father, inviting nods of approval from his men. 'We'll make farmers of you all!'

As he said this, Brinie dropped a bundle and cried out. Like everyone else, I snapped my attention towards her. She was shaking her hand and at first I thought she had been stung. Then I saw a dark shape attached to the webbing between her thumb and fore-finger, and yet more scattering across the floor.

A moment later, those shapes seemed to regroup like flocking birds and swarmed upon her friend. Kath twisted around with a piercing shriek, flapping her hands with her face contorted. Dad and some of the men were upon the rats in a moment, snatching them away while the dogs did a fine job of dispatching them. It was a moment that began in shock and horror, but ended seconds later in silence. With the last rat finished, Kath faced us all in turn while doing a heroic job of holding back her tears. Brinie was the only one to make a sound, muttering darkly as she nursed her nipped hand. Finally, Kath found my father and addressed him directly. 'May I go home now?' she asked in a very quiet voice indeed.

'Not without a hot cup of tea and a slice of cake in the farm-house,' he said, and beckoned me down from the thresher. 'Joan, take these young heroines inside and show them how grateful we are.' He gestured towards the sacks of grain that had been gathered from the thresher. 'We couldn't have done this without you, girls. You're a credit to the nation, and that's exactly what I shall tell the nurses, Brinie, when I drive you back via the hospital so they can take a look at that hand.'

'I'll be fine,' said Brinie, but my father insisted.

'I always take care of my crew,' he told her.

Soon after the rats, in the spring of the following year, another front opened out on the fields. Like the vermin, it was just another aspect of life at Quarry Pits. Every year the seasons would bring a different challenge. Sometimes, however, that challenge would threaten to disrupt the crops or livestock, and then it had to be tackled as a priority. On this occasion, with Dad so busy with the planting, it fell to me to deal with it.

'It's time your ferrets earned their keep,' he said to me one evening as I joined him on his way back to the farmhouse.

I knew just what he was talking about. With the sun setting, the field that sloped away from the cherry orchard was spotted with rabbits. They were everywhere, having surfaced from a warren that looked bigger than ever before.

'Consider it done,' I said, eager to help.

'Get Swanker Jones's boy to lend you a hand,' he added, though I already had him in mind.

Swanker Jones was a familiar face on the doorsteps of households across Dormston. A man who knew how to winkle money from your purse with his charm alone, he worked from a cart and dray piled high with vegetables from his farm. Now Swanker had a son called David with a gift for catching rabbits. It meant he often carried a brace for the pot, and offered his lad's services to anyone who was overrun.

It was David Jones who suggested we should use ferrets to help keep the rabbit population under control at Quarry Pits. I housed two in a cage in the scullery. I cared for them in every way, but they weren't pets. The white one was friendly enough, and I was happy to slip her into my trouser leg when I set out with David that evening. The other ferret, a Fitch, with a dark pelt and white mask across its face, was a nasty brute with quite a bite, and I carried him out in a sack.

'He might be mean,' said David, 'but he'll do you right tonight.'

He was much older than me, and though he didn't speak much he was keen to show me his craft. David taught me how to set a snare, which is a skill I have never forgotten, and also how to lay out nets across a warren before we set about flushing out the occupants. This was where the ferrets came alive. Each one was fitted with a collar with a long length of string attached, and then sent into the burrow. That evening, I set the white one to work while David handled the Fitch.

'How many do you think we'll get?' I asked.

'Half a dozen?' he replied, which sounded like a guess, but an educated one at that.

I watched the white ferret sniff the excavated soil and then disappear from view. Carefully, I let the string unwind and hoped it wouldn't snag or become entangled on a tree root. Sometimes, if that happened, you had to just let go of the string and hope the animal freed itself. Otherwise, you'd have to dig it out, and that could take all night. Once, I'd lost the white one in a burrow and been forced to give her up for dead. I tried to be grown up about it, but the child in me took over back at the farmhouse and I wept myself to sleep. Two days later, Marian had found her stretched out beside the Aga, sleeping off what must've been quite an adventure.

'And they're off!' declared David, racing for a rabbit that had just launched straight into a net. A moment later, another one popped up nearby, followed by a third and then a fourth. They surfaced so fast, flushed out by the ferrets, we could barely keep up. An hour later, with our sleek and efficient hunters safely back in my care, I walked back to the farmhouse under a sickle moon and with my head held high. David followed close behind, struggling to keep the stick balanced over his shoulder what with the weight of the catch strung from it. We had caught up to twenty rabbits that evening. It was a record never bettered by my father, or by David, who repeated that story in the pub snug for many years to come.

PART TWO

12

Man's Land

I always enjoyed the ploughing competitions.

I was seven years old when war broke out, and thirteen when it finally came to an end. A shroud of darkness had fallen over my childhood, but I never let it stop me make the most of my time growing up. There were hardships and difficulties, of course, but the experience shaped the person I am today. When light broke out across the world once more, I had learned to farm the land just like my father, and had become a young woman with my whole life ahead of me.

In those post-war years, as I became more useful around Quarry Pits, I also started to flex my wings. In what free time I had, I began to enter ploughing matches. With John in tow, I would venture out around the county and often further afield to take part in competitions. Autumn was the season that saw us take off at weekends.

You might not think there's much involved in preparing a field for planting out, but the farming community take it very seriously. We'd arrive to join up to forty competitors at a time. Brother and

I got to know lots of them, but rivalry was fierce. I only had to catch someone's eye to see them sizing me up. I'm sure they took one look and wonder what a girl like me was doing in a challenge that demanded both muscle and precision, but I soon showed them.

With the field divided up into plots, and spectators crowding around, each competitor would go to work. First, I'd mark out the furrows. This would give me a chance to assess the soil. I was used to the heavy clay ground of Quarry Pits. 'Man's Land', we called it. The kind of land that was tough to farm, but I knew how to make the most of it. Naturally, everyone preferred 'Boy's Land'; the sandy soil you could scoop into the palm of your hand and crumble with your fingers.

Of course, the weather also influenced how deep I'd set the ploughshare. It could make the difference between turning ground that was wet as a bog or baked hard.

Working within a set time, we were judged on all manner of factors, from the straightness of the furrows to the neatness of the turns at the end of each field. Brother and I were competitive like everyone else, but also hugely supportive, and I took pride in the fact that he learned so many of his skills from me. By the time he turned fifteen, however, having shot up like a weed and broadened in the chest, John began to win in his class. Finally, when he joined me in the adult category, he would go on to beat me hands down. Every time he received a rosette or a trophy, nobody would be clapping louder than me. There's nothing better than teaching someone the basics of a craft and then watching them take off to exceed all expectation. Mastering any discipline, from ploughing to riding a horse, brings out their true spirit, I think, and if I'm responsible for setting that in motion then it's a job well done. In return for my efforts with John, he looked out for me. He would often offer to be my chaperone, in fact, when I started going out to social events and dances at weekends.

Nothing, however, compared to my father's watchful eye.

If I were to show my left hand, you'd see a fine scar just behind one of the knuckles. This was the result of an accident I once suffered while trimming a hedgerow at Quarry Pits, aged seventeen or so. Fortunately, the doctors saved the finger and that scar serves to remind me of my time growing up at the farm. It was an age in which I learned to get on no matter what misfortune we faced. Even so, for a brief time I wondered if I might never have the chance to see a man slip a ring upon that finger.

I certainly didn't pay much interest in boys for quite some time. There was just too much work to be done on the farm, with different seasons bringing fresh demands. I made plenty of friends at school, at course, and enjoyed spending time out with girls like Thelma, Mary, Rita, Carol, Jennifer and Pat. We'd go dancing and all sorts, which is when John would accompany me. I wasn't shy around the opposite sex, and of course I became curious about the idea of romance. It really was just a question of priorities, and the farm always came first. It had to. I could often find a spare evening or Sunday to go out, of course, but I wasn't sure I wanted to lose my heart to someone when I felt so happy in the fields. It struck me as a distraction, though nobody forced me to work. Mother often talked about certain sons of her friends in such a way that I knew she was sounding me out, but I did nothing to encourage her. Still, she seemed very pleased when I finally took a shine to a nice young man who had asked to call upon me, while John offered to cover my tasks on the farm so I didn't have to worry. They looked forward to meeting him, in fact; the boy who had finally turned Joan's eye. What we hadn't considered, however, was that the poor fellow would have to face my father. Colin Collins had no issue with his daughter courting, but his standards were as exacting as they could be uncompromising.

It meant if my Dad took a dislike to my suitor in any way, as happened to poor George Smith, he'd never even make it to the front door.

George was a local boy. A personable young lad who worked on a nearby farm, but was always in a hurry. One time, behind the wheel of a tractor, he towed a threshing machine between gates that weren't quite wide enough. News of the episode, and the damage done to both the gate and the machine, quickly spread around the area.

'That boy needs to slow down,' my dad said when he heard about it. 'That's how people get hurt.'

Now, I liked George. He was shy at first, but had a lovely smile and wasn't afraid of hard work. He blushed so hard when he braved asking if I'd like to spend one Sunday in his company, but I accepted straight away. It felt lovely to be invited, and I remember working with a spring in my step in the days preceding our date.

George made a special effort that day. He dressed smartly, and had every intention of treating me with kindness and respect. Unfortunately for him, no doubt recalling that incident with the thresher, Father wasn't prepared to let him risk making any mistakes with me. Being a man of few words outside of his family and crew, my dad took it upon himself to express himself with a gesture that left no room for misunderstanding.

George almost certainly would have carried some nerves in his gut as he strode along the lane towards Quarry Pits. It takes courage to ask someone out, after all. But what he encountered next must've caused his heart to quicken for all the wrong reasons. As the bathroom window opened, the glare of the sun on the glass drew his attention. He peered up, just as my dad appeared in the frame. Doubtless George also caught sight of the shotgun resting across the ledge. I imagine Father made every effort to make sure that he saw it.

'Good afternoon, Mr Collins!' he called up to him, mindful of his manners. 'Shooting wood pigeons?'

In response, and without a word, my dad calmly picked up the gun, braced the stock against his shoulder and took aim directly at George. The boy froze, the smile withering on his face, and then watched in disbelief as Father lifted the muzzle to the sky and let off a round. Needless to say, George didn't hang around to see if he planned to use the other barrell. Like the birds in the surrounding trees, George took flight with the sound of that shot still crackling away over the fields. I'm told he didn't stop running until he reached Inkberrow, and that was the end of our romance before it had even begun.

Sometime later, once it became clear that George no longer presented a threat to his daughter's future, Father revised his attitude towards him. Most surprisingly of all, he even employed him at Quarry Pits. George drove his tractor, too, which was a sure sign that Dad had learned to trust him, and he would go on to be a family friend for decades. They never spoke about the incident with the shotgun, but I suspect in some ways it bonded them.

Father was certainly vigilant, but one or two boys managed to take me out without his knowledge. In some ways, I wish he'd been there to stop me from a blind date with a trainee dentist from Evesham. It was a disaster because, frankly, we had nothing in common. We might as well have been speaking a different language. All he could talk about was root canal work and brushing technique, and he had no interest in anything I had to say. I'd honestly rather have had a tooth extracted by him than have had to endure that painful supper, but it was a day out on the back of a motorcycle with a boy from Redditch that put me off boys for a while. Somehow, he had managed to pick me up without Dad's knowledge, and whisked me off for a road trip. I can't recall where we went as I had my eyes squeezed shut for most of it. Travelling back, with my arms wrapped around his waist for dear life as we roared through country lanes, I dared to peep over his shoulder and saw the speed-ometer needle heading towards one hundred miles per hour. I vowed that if he delivered me back to Quarry Pits in one piece I would never see that man again, and I remained true to my word.

Everyone adored Bill Hilson, the son of the local iron foundry owner, and that included my dad. We bought our ploughshares from his father, and the quality of his work was second to none. Bill served as his apprentice. There was just something about the boy's nature that Father appreciated, and I was enormously fond of him.

Bill and I went out several times. He was prompt to arrive and would always deliver me home safely and at a good hour. I had even begun to wonder whether perhaps we would settle down together, and build a life of our own. So when Bill failed to show up one day, with no call to explain his absence, I couldn't hide my disappointment. To take my mind off things, John badgered me to help him sweep out the barn, but inside I felt so sad and let down.

Several days passed before we discovered what had happened, and it left me distraught. The night before we were due to spend the day together, Bill had been hard at work in his father's foundry workshop. He was determined to learn the trade, and earn the same reputation as his dad. Nobody knows what happened for sure. We can only think he had been trying to move a heavy lathe when it fell on him and took his life. That poor young man had so much to give, only for it to be snatched away. It took me a long while to get over the loss, and I couldn't have done it without the support of my family. As farmers, we were used to difficult times, and knew we would find a way to get through them no matter what. While the challenges we faced were typically rooted in the land, however, this was a crisis of the heart. Even so, my parents and siblings supported me through that chapter with just the same conviction that life would see me right, and I loved them for it.

13
Young Farmers

A Young Farmers dinner.

When I was twelve, my dad took me to a club meeting at the village hall. It was a weekly event, and something the lads in his crew would often talk about with great affection. As a child, working alongside them, I heard stories about the fun and games enjoyed by the members that made me laugh out loud, while I longed to forge the kind of friendships and camaraderie that so clearly bonded them in a special kind of family. So when Father suggested that I was old enough to enrol, I arrived knowing that I was about to join a world that would come to mean an enormous amount to me: The Young Farmers.

In those days, with local communication limited to telephone and hearsay, the club served as a vital social network. Anyone up to the age of twenty-six who had a connection with the land was welcome. Across Inkberrow and Dormston, that pretty much accounted for an entire generation within our community.

In my early years as a club member, I looked up to many young farmers, and aspired to be like them. John would join me just as soon as he was old enough, and by then I had made some good mates. Of course, the war meant many of the young men left to fight. Although brave men like Alfred Strain, David Parker and Sidney Ballard did not return, the club endured and thrived once the conflict ended. From agricultural classes and practical instruction to proficiency tests and awards, as well as competitions and supper dances, there was always something happening that I looked forward to. Travelling to and from the hall on our bicycles, over the course of a decade it became a second home.

'Make sure your bike lamps are working before you set off,' Mum often reminded us whenever the clocks went back and the moon was on the wax or wane. 'Otherwise it might not just be Father you'll answer to.'

We used carbide lights in those days. These were handy little devices with two chambers behind the lamp that combined water with calcium carbide powder and burned brightly as acetylene. I always made sure that both chambers on my lamp were topped up. Out in the Vale of Evesham, on country lanes after dark, it could become pitch black at times. What's more, while the local bobby left most people to get on with their lives, he was a stickler for the rules when it came to road regulations around the village, and that's just who my mother had in mind.

PC Dudfield had been our village policeman for a long time. He was a big man who enjoyed a joke so long as it wasn't at his expense. As we lived in a quiet and peaceful community, he was just one more friendly face with no reason to cause us problems. One time, however my father was faced with a small conundrum. He'd contracted out his steam tackle and crew to a farm on the other side of the village. Work had taken longer than planned, and nightfall set in. As a result, he was looking at negotiating two engines, a plough and a water cart on country lanes after dark. Even with lamps, he knew that PC Dudfield would regard that kind of convoy as a dangerous load. With commitments the next day, however, my dad decided that he had no choice. As a precaution, having set his lads off to Quarry Pits with the tackle, Father headed down to the police station with me.

Inside, PC Dudfield stood behind the desk as if he'd been squashed in there. He seemed surprised to see us, and that quickly turned to suspicion when Dad began spinning some tall story about the threat of cattle rustlers from across the Vale. I remember standing at his side as a distant but familiar rumbling sound began to underscore their conversation. Even PC Dudfield seemed to register it, but Dad just pressed him hard about what precautionary measures the police might take. At one point, I glanced through the side window. Across the field, between the trees that defined the back lane there, I could plainly see a lumbering caravan of agricultural machinery trundling under the moonlight. Dad kept the man's attention, however, and only wished him goodnight when the night returned to silence.

'Mr Collins,' he called after us, just as we reached the door. I glanced up at Dad, and turned with him to face the desk. PC Dudfield no longer looked suspicious. Instead, he regarded us with bridled indignation. 'I know what you're doing out there, you know? And if I catch anyone travelling without lights in future, there will be hell to pay!'

As much as the story amused his men when we shared it with them the next day, Dad took the officer's warning very seriously. We had pushed our luck, he decided, and from there on out it was only right that his family used the lanes to the letter of the law.

So, with our bike lamps glowing, John and I would peddle into the village once a week to meet up with people our age who would one day become farmers in their own right.

Naturally, with young men and women mixing socially, romances were quick to form. Even though that never worked out for me, I adored spending time with individuals who had grown up just as I had and shared the same values. I wasn't silly as a young woman. I never lost my head, but I liked to laugh and unwind with friends after a hard week's work. We became a tight bunch, and never was this more apparent than the evening Michael Farquhar braved cycling home with empty chambers in his carbide lamp.

'Old Dudfield is out there, you know?' warned one of the young farmers as Michael prepared to leave. 'I saw him pedalling past the pub on the way here.'

'Then let's hope he stopped for a pint,' quipped Michael. 'Besides, it's dark out there. My bike has no light. He'll never see me!'

Michael Farquhar was one of the older members. He was confident and fun to be around, and I had just beaten him at cards. We'd been enjoying a whist drive that evening. Both John and I enjoyed those sessions immensely. As a game it was always fun, but I liked the fact that each round saw players switching tables, which meant I had a chance to spend time with everyone.

'Be careful,' I said as he squeezed behind my chair.

'You don't need to worry about me.' Michael patted me on the shoulder. 'You just make sure you get home safely.'

'You don't have to worry about me either,' I chuckled, and gestured at my brother at a table across the room.

Michael grinned at me from over his shoulder and headed for the door. I looked at the clock on the wall. There was just enough time to play one more round before the warden closed the hall for the evening, and so I rose to find another table.

Ten minutes later, midway through my final game, the door to the hall banged open. Like everyone else, startled by the crashing sound that followed, I gasped and rose to my feet.

'*Make way!*' yelled a familiar voice. '*Coming through!*'

It took a moment for me to register the figure on the bicycle. Somehow, Michael Farquhar had retained his balance after such a dramatic entrance, and now pedalled furiously between the tables.

'What on earth are you doing?' asked one lad, who like everyone else seemed unsure whether to laugh or be outraged. 'Michael, have you lost your marbles?'

'There's only one thing I want to lose right now,' he called back, freewheeling as he weaved towards the exit door at the back, and clearly relishing the drama. 'If he asks after me, I trust you'll say the right thing!'

Leaving the group to stare at one another dumbfounded, Michael dismounted briefly to negotiate the exit, before cycling furiously into the night. I couldn't be sure what direction he took, across the little green back there or the lane adjacent. Without a light, he just seemed to be swallowed up by darkness.

'I've seen some things,' declared one of the young farmers, stunned like all of us. 'That's going to take some beating!'

Even before he'd drawn breath, another bicycle rider clattered through the entrance into the hall.

'Where did he go?' yelled PC Dudfield. 'I saw him slip in here. Come out, you cheeky beggar!'

Most of us were still on our feet. This time, nobody laughed. PC Dudfield dismounted, his face puce from what had clearly been a frantic pursuit, and looked around.

'Who are you looking for, officer?' asked one chap. He had gathered his composure wonderfully, unlike so many others, and simply faced PC Dudfield as if nothing untoward had just happened.

'You know full well,' growled the officer, his face growing redder despite his having come to rest. 'The lad, Michael. The boy I've just seen cycling merrily through the high street with no lights. I demanded that he stop and he scarpered. Is he here?'

Despite the fury in the policeman's voice, and the gravity of the situation, I caught Brother's eye and he pulled a face. Let me tell you, I was trying so hard not to laugh. I must've squeaked because PC Dudfield looked around. Well aware that he knew me by name, and no doubt hadn't forgotten his encounter with my father, I looked to my shoes.

'There's no lad called Michael here,' said a voice from a nearby table. 'Does anyone know a Michael?' he added, to much shaking of heads and mutterings that the policeman must be mistaken.

I dared to look up once more. Clutching his handlebars, PC

Dudfield looked as furious as he did breathless, and then turned his attention to the exit door. It was still ajar, knocking lightly in the breeze as if to summon his attention.

'This will not be forgotten.' With his knuckles whitening, the indignant bobby gripped the handlebars of his bike and pushed on towards the door. 'Get out of my way,' he grumbled, causing several young farmers to clear his path as he heaved himself back into the saddle. 'This is an emergency!'

For a moment, as he pedalled furiously from the hall, everyone just stood in silence. Then someone chuckled, and the place erupted. It was one of the most memorable nights of my time with the Young Farmers, and one that still held some adventure for me. For with all the drama and laughter that followed, John and I clean forgot the time.

Father was quite happy for Brother and I to spend evenings out, but Mother didn't relax until we were home. As a result, he always set a time for us to be back. Even though they turned in early, it was a rule that could not be broken.

That evening, any villager who was still out at that late hour would've seen two carbine lamps switching wildly along the lane out of Inkberrow.

'You know what Dad can be like,' John said as we sailed down the incline. 'He'll be listening out for that kitchen door to creak open, and we'll be for it!'

'Then we'll find another way in,' I said, and prepared to pedal hard as the lane levelled off.

We dismounted within sight of Quarry Pits, and extinguished our lamps. Then, with the bikes stowed away, I crept around the garden wall with John following close behind. Under the boughs of the horse chestnut, I eased open the back gate and signalled for him to follow me across the lawn towards the house.

'There's no way we can climb up to our bedrooms,' he hissed, pulling me back, but I had other plans.

'Who said anything about climbing up?' I gestured at the recessed window that formed the light well for the cellar. Father always left it ajar so the air didn't get stale down there.

John grinned at me.

'When are you going to stop clambering into tight spaces?' he asked, as I prepared to squeeze in head first.

'Never,' I told my dear brother from the other side, and helped him through before we made our way to bed without disturbing a soul.

14

Two is Company

A brief rest before getting back to work.

'There's a lad wants to see you,' Mother announced to Marian one day. My sister had been helping out in the kitchen. I was preparing to work in the barn, but couldn't help overhearing our mum explain that the boy's mother was looking for someone responsible to accompany her son on a forthcoming trip, and Mother had suggested my sister.

'Oh, I don't know,' Marian said, flattered by the invitation but also flustered. 'I have so much work to do here.'

'Who is he?' I asked on making my way to the door. 'Is he nice?'

Tony Bomford was the son of another local farming family. They lived just over fourteen miles away at South Littleton, in a handsome white house amid a broad expanse of cattle fields, elm and wild hedgerow. I hadn't met Tony, but our parents were on familiar terms with his mother and father. As dairy farmers, the Bomfords had made quite a success of things up there.

'Tony is set to go on a trip with the Friesian Breeders Club,' Mum said, still pressing Marian. 'I suggested that you'd make a lovely companion.' She added, 'Why don't you just meet him?'

I didn't have much in common with my sister, but we shared the same strong work ethic. While my interests lay outside the farmhouse door, in the fields, the yard and the barn, my sister continued to divide her time between her academic studies and the housekeeping duties that she genuinely adored. It gave her a sense of purpose and pride, and I understood that. Like our brother, John, I just pursued the same values working outside in the fresh air.

That's exactly what I was doing a few days later when the young man first approached the farmhouse. Father had asked me to oversee the cleaning of the threshing machine, which needed regular attention to stop it from becoming clogged by all the grain and chaff it processed. It was a warm, bright day, and we'd set to work on it just outside the blacksmith's workshop.

'Excuse me,' he said, which first drew my attention to his presence. 'Would you be Marian Collins by any chance?'

This caused some of the men with me to chuckle, but I just wiped my brow with the back of my hand and told him where to find her. He looked very embarrassed, and a little lost for words, and so I introduced myself.

'I'm Tony,' he said in response and shook my hand despite it being so grubby. He was a handsome young man, one year younger than me at nineteen, with a dark wedge of hair cut short at the sides. Above all, what struck me was his boyish smile. 'So,' he said, and gestured at the machine behind me. 'What are you doing?'

I was standing with an oily rag slung over my shoulder and my sleeves rolled to the elbow, while the men behind me worked to remove the elevator belt so we could clean underneath it. I was tempted to scoff, but reminded myself of my manners. It was also clear to me that a farmer's son would know full well that a thresher demanded regular maintenance, and that his nerves had just got the better of him. As soon as he asked the question, in fact, he looked to the ground as if hoping a hole might crack open and swallow him up.

'You'll find Marian and my mother in the kitchen,' I said instead, hoping to spare him further blushes. 'I hope you like cake.'

Tony Bomford looked up and caught my eye. I smiled and so did he.

Later that day, with the thresher cleaned and reassembled, I headed inside for a glass of water. I found Marian in the kitchen, polishing the cutlery.

'So?' I asked her. 'Are you going on the tour with Tony? He seems very nice.'

'He is,' she agreed, but without much interest in my question. 'But he's asked if he can go with you.'

I didn't agree straight away. Marian was absolutely fine about it. She seemed relieved, in fact, and encouraged me to go. I wasn't so sure, however, even after Mother came to terms with the fact that her eldest was out of the running. Accompanying that young man and his club on a tour of cow farms seemed appealing at one level, but frankly I had too much to do at Quarry Pits. It was Father who persuaded me to accept. He assured me that they'd manage, and kept saying what an opportunity it would be to see how other farms took care of their livestock.

'I'm beginning to think you want to get rid of me!' I joked at one point, after he raised the subject again while we were out in the fields.

'I'd have you working alongside me for the rest of my days,' he said, and paused to lean on his pitchfork. 'Quarry Pits will always be your home, as it is for Marian and John, but this is an opportunity to see what's out there.'

'I'm not so sure,' I said warily.

The sun was in and out that day, and had just emerged from

behind clouds that threatened rain. Father looked up, cupping his brow at the same time.

'We should be getting on,' he said. 'While the weather is with us.'

Having first proposed that Marian would make an ideal companion for Tony on his trip, Mother made every effort to persuade me to take up his invitation.

'He sees something in you,' she said, and then broke into a smile. 'And I hope you see something in a fine young man like him.'

'What about Marian?' I asked.

Mother looked at me like she'd expected the question. I was concerned, of course, for Tony had visited the house to meet my sister, not me.

'She thinks you make a good pair,' said Mum. 'We both do.'

Eventually, I agreed to pack a bag. I would only be gone for a few days, my dad pointed out. Although he wasn't quite as keen as Marian and Mum, he recognised that Tony was a nice young man at heart who would be sure to look after me. I reminded him that I didn't need looking after, and just hoped the two of us would have enough to talk about to get through the trip.

On the day the tour was due to begin, Father drove me out to the turnpike opposite the post box. The party from the Friesian Breeders Club was travelling by coach. Tony had arranged for the driver to stop there to collect me, and that was where I asked myself if I was doing the right thing.

'Dad,' I said, as he carried my case from the car.

I didn't need to say any more. The plaintive tone in which I'd addressed him spoke volumes. He just looked at me like he'd been expecting this moment since we set off from the farm.

'Everything will be fine,' he assured me, grasping me by the shoulders.

'But he's a year younger than I am!' It was all I could think to say. The only reason I could come up with at that moment as to why I should cancel, and it simply made him chuckle.

'Then *you* should look after *him*!' he said.

A moment later, Father glanced over his shoulder as the coach pulled up behind his car. 'Go and enjoy yourself, Joan,' he said, as Tony jumped out to greet me. 'Quarry Pits will still be standing when you come back.'

On my return, five days later, Dad asked all about the tour. He wanted details of the cattle farms we had visited and the different methods they employed in caring for their herds, but talk of Tony went unspoken. As I told Mother and my sister, however, he had turned out to be good company. Unlike my previous dates, we'd had a lot in common and plenty to talk about. We had conducted our time together on a friendly basis, and I had enjoyed myself thoroughly. I was pleased to be home, but I also looked forward to seeing him again.

It would be several weeks before Tony called me on our new telephone. In that time, I had quietly hoped that he would ring. At the same time, I threw myself into work on the farm and helping out Dad where possible. So when he finally made contact I was a little bit cool with him. Did I want to go to the pictures, he asked? I might, I told him, simple as that, but didn't argue when he took that as confirmation.

To this day, I will never know why Tony thought it would be a good idea to invite his old flame, Margaret, to accompany us. I can only think he was just being friendly, because that was central to his nature, though looking back his mother might've had a hand in it. Marian might've appealed to her as the model of domesticity, whereas I was just a girl who got in the way of men's work. Margaret, on the other hand, was the vicar's daughter. She possessed the same qualities as my sister, but with some social standing, and I have no doubt that Tony would've been encouraged to bring her along for the ride. Still, the poor lad looked genuinely puzzled after pulling up to collect me, when I took one look at the passenger and called off the date.

'Two is company,' I told him, before turning my back on him so he couldn't see my face fall. 'But three is a crowd!'

It wasn't long before he called me to apologise, and ask me out again. I declined his invitation because I didn't like being hurt, and though he might've been foolish he was at least persistent. After a few months of his calling me every now and then, I agreed to go to the pictures with him. There was just one condition, as I made clear on the phone. If we were going to enjoy an evening out then the only company I expected was his. By then, enough time had passed for us both to see the funny side, and that's when romance blossomed.

Tony was a quiet man, just like my dad in many ways. He was principled and intelligent, but liked to be in familiar company before he spoke freely. An only child, he had been sent to boarding school before being called up for national service with the air force. Working as a switchboard operator did little to inspire him, however. He would come home on leave, show his pass to the railway station master − who, on one occasion, was busy soaking his corns in a bucket of water − and realise how much he missed country life. Then his father had fallen ill, and Tony seized the opportunity to return to take care of the farm. He was quite content in his calling, working in partnership with his dad once he recovered. Even so, he longed for the kind of family life that I enjoyed, and which he felt that he had missed out on.

Tony and I began to see each other regularly. First, we went out on dates and then just spent time together doing everyday things. Sometimes he would help me on the farm, and I enjoyed his company. He was a good worker, Tony, and that earned my dad's respect. As we grew to relax with each other, he certainly came out of his shell. That shy, boyish smile soon broadened, and he revealed a sense of humour that could make me laugh and laugh. He helped to build my confidence, too, and once I'd encouraged him to join me at my Young Farmers meetings we became inseparable.

In the summer of my twentieth year, Tony went down on one

knee and presented a ring to me. We were in a field at the time, assessing the hay for harvest. I couldn't think of a more appropriate place, and nor could he. I took a breath when he proposed and then held it for a moment.

'I'll think about it,' I said eventually.

Tony rose to his feet, as stunned at what he had just put himself through as he was by my response.

'What does that mean?' he asked, pawing anxiously at the back of his neck.

'It means just that,' I said, and reminded him that we had a job to do.

I loved him deeply. That wasn't an issue. But I also loved my life at Quarry Pits. I just wasn't sure I wanted to give it up, so I left Tony waiting for a week before I gave him an answer.

My decision came after a day helping Father with the cows. He knew I was torn about the proposal, but didn't press me to talk about it. In fact, my dad was the same as he ever was, just focused on the job at hand, and that helped me to make sense of everything. As a farmer's daughter, I had been raised to recognise that hard work could provide stability through each season, and a foundation for happiness. Now I'd met a dear man who was offering me the chance to bring these values into a marriage, and even create a family of my own. As I watched my dad, I realised that nothing could take away the blessed start I'd had in life. It would always be there as something I could build upon. So, when Tony braved pressing me for an answer, I broke into a heartfelt smile and told him I would be honoured to become his wife.

'So … you want to marry me?' he asked to clarify, as if perhaps he'd braced himself for bad news.

'Yes,' I said. 'I do.'

15

Flight of Fancy

Our wedding day in August 1954.

My mother told a story when my siblings and I were young that will no doubt pass through the generations. It concerns my father on his wedding day, and sums up the character of the family that I was born into.

Colin Collins was a man in love. There is no doubt about that. He knew that Kitty was the woman for him. She'd been born and raised into a farming family, and embraced his way of life. And yet when the day of the wedding arrived my dad was an unsettled soul. As he buttoned himself into his morning suit, and struggled with his tie, he considered his reflection in the mirror. The prospect of saying his vows before God didn't trouble him. It was the thought of being seen dressed up in such finery.

'Look at you,' he muttered to himself. 'Who do you think you are?'

Throughout his life, Father had dressed practically. In his muddy boots, trousers, braces and a shirt, plus the cap that rarely left his head, he was a familiar sight on the fields and in the lanes at the helm of a steam convoy. Imagining himself striding out to the church in polished shoes that squeaked just made him grimace. For someone who could happily spend days without seeing anyone but his family and crew, it was just too much for him to bear.

And so my dad set off for the ceremony in good time, but took the only route that helped him feel comfortable. Instead of following the lane, he headed for the stile across from Quarry Pits and made his way up the field. It was a route that would take him through woodland, where he could be quite sure that only squirrels and deer would register his presence. Finally, feeling very pleased that he had made the journey undetected, Father emerged from the trees and over the wall into the cemetery behind the church, brushed himself down and made his way around to the entrance.

I can't say why my dad failed to consider the fact that every pew would be filled with friends, family and villagers awaiting his arrival, but he took one look at the congregation and very nearly turned tail. By then, however, with everyone facing him, he reminded himself of the reason why he was there. Calling upon every last drop of courage in his body, he lifted his chin and took up position at the front of the church to await his beautiful bride-to-be.

It's an episode from my dad's life that still makes me chuckle. Then I reflect on the run-up to my own wedding, and realise that we were cut from the same cloth in so many ways.

Tony and I were engaged for a year, and set our wedding date for August 1954. Quarry Pits was thriving as a cattle farm, and while agricultural technology had advanced, my dad still found his con-tracting services in demand. We had a wedding to plan, and yet the farm took up all my time. As Tony continued to play a central role in managing his own family's livestock, we just seized whatever moments we could find to prepare for our big day.

As a result, I didn't give it much thought. The wedding was just another date in the farm diary. One that required planning and preparation just like the ploughing, seeding and harvesting of a field. Between us, we drew up a list of all the things that needed doing, from sending out the invitations to preparing the village hall for our reception, and simply got on with it. Together with Mother and Marian, who came into her own in supporting me, we even did all the catering ourselves. As the day grew nearer, so I found my time was even more hard pressed in order to make sure that everything would be ready. It was only on the morning of my wedding, in fact, that I finally paused for thought.

Up until that moment, I'd been busy running around ticking things off my list. I had just found the sandwiches beautifully arranged on plates in the kitchen, as Mother had promised. She had also laid out the pastries on a tray beside them, and covered everything for the short journey to the village hall.

'I'll take them in Dad's car,' I said, for he had recently permitted me to drive his beloved old Wolseley.

'Do you have time?' asked Marian, wiping flour from her palms on her apron. 'What about your wedding dress?'

'It won't take me long to get ready,' I assured her, and began ferrying the plates to the car.

I had enjoyed completing each task as the day approached. Now it had arrived, and with this last chore outstanding, I felt a little out of sorts. Steering the car out onto the lane, I began to think about the ceremony. Tony would be there on time, without a doubt, the floral arrangements in place and every pew filled.

The only thing missing from that scene in my mind, I thought, on setting off for the village hall, was me.

Just then, for a split second, I asked myself whether I was doing the right thing. In the car's mirror, I could still see Quarry Pits. There it stood at the foot of the rise, overlooking the low-lying fields, the woods and meadows. I knew every square foot of that one-hundred-acre world, and now here I was set to leave it all behind. I had already come to terms with the fact that it was time for me to move on. I just questioned whether I was heading in the right direction. I focused on the lane once again, and wondered what would happen if I just pressed the accelerator and kept on going. I could put the hall behind me in minutes, heading for the open road. But it wasn't genuine doubt that had come into my mind; I knew that straight away. It was just a final, fleeting flight of fancy, and it vanished in a blink.

As soon as I neared the village hall, I knew deep down that I had made the right decision. My future lay with Tony. I loved him, and wanted to share the rest of our lives together. It was an uncertain time, of course. I was giving up the sense of stability my family had worked hard to sustain, but then I had faith that my new husband and I could make it work. Had I driven on, I reflected, once I'd had a moment to consider it, I would've simply got lost.

'Where have you been? Look at the time!'

Mother looked both relieved and stricken when I finally returned home from the hall several hours after I'd set off. Having delivered the sandwiches, I'd stayed to make sure everything looked just right. From the centrepieces to the refreshments table, I checked everything with the same care that I would show a threshing machine or Fowler engine. There's no point half doing things if you want to get a job done properly. That's always been my outlook on life, and I applied it to my own wedding. Even so, it still felt strange to think that all the preparations were for me to take centre stage. Marian had already got ready. She looked so elegant as a bridesmaid, while I was still in work clothes.

'I'll help you with your dress,' my sister said. 'As the bride you're expected to be late, but not too late!'

'We'll get there on time,' I told her. 'All I have to do is change out of these old things.'

Marian and Mother looked equally appalled.

'Joan, it's your wedding day!' my mum reminded me. 'This is a once in a lifetime experience. Surely you want to treasure every second?'

I looked at them both with a smile on my face. It was amusing to see them like this, and I really didn't understand what all the fuss was about.

'Five minutes is all I need,' I insisted, chuckling as I headed for the hallway and the stairs. 'I can manage quite capably by myself!'

I had tried on the dress for size several weeks earlier. At the time, with such lovely sunshine streaming through the window, all I had wanted to do was hurry up so I could get back outside. I was distracted, and happy to let Marian fuss around making all the necessary adjustments. It meant when I unhooked it from the wardrobe door just then, where Mother had left it waiting for me, it felt like I was about to wear it for the very first time.

As a young woman who always liked to keep her promise, I reappeared in the kitchen within a matter of minutes. Father had joined my mum and older sister now. All three faced me as I asked them how I looked, and they blinked as I just stood there.

'Well?' I said, and twisted at the waist so they could appraise me.

'That'll do,' said Father, only to stop at a catch in his voice. He cleared his throat, turning from me at the same time, which left me with Mother and Marian.

'Is that all the time you need?' Mother glanced at the clock on the wall. 'Joan, you look lovely, but you can have a little longer if you like.'

As well as climbing into my dress, I'd even had time to apply some makeup and brush my hair. I didn't want to fiddle around too much. I wanted to look like me.

'I'm ready as I am,' I said, as Father recovered his composure and faced me once again. 'And may I say how smart you're looking,' I added, admiring the suit that Mother had brought out of mothballs for him.

Father shot his cuffs and sighed.

'As much as it's an honour to be giving away my daughter,' he said, 'I can't wait to get back into my normal clothes.'

'Same here,' I said, beaming brightly, and invited him to escort me up the slope to where my wedding car awaited.

The service was lovely. In front of family and friends, with John, Marian and my parents looking on proudly, Tony and I exchanged our vows. Any uncertainties or wobbles that I might've had since he asked for my hand just melted away. Tony was a man I could trust. A kindred spirit in many ways, and not just because we came from farming families. I was so happy, and it made my day to see the people I loved share in that joy. After the ceremony, we headed for the village hall where at last I began to relax. The speeches were heart-warming, funny and kind, and I was pleased to see that all our hard work with the catering went down so well.

'I'm glad you made it,' said Tony at one point, from our seat at the top table.

'Were you worried?' I asked, beaming as I had been since I first walked into the church.

Tony faced me, and took my hand.

'I recognise what you've given up in choosing to be with me, Joan. And I promise you that I won't let you down.'

When I look at pictures of our wedding day, I see everyone smiling and enjoying what proved to be a delightful occasion for friends as much as family. They're mostly formal shots, as was commonplace in those days, and yet even with everyone taking their positions for the photographer it's clear that laughter fills the air. There are shots of Father and Brother looking almost unrecognisable in suits and having put a comb through their hair, but standing proud as punch. Mum truly shone on that day, and no doubt she was filled with memories of her own wedding. And yet there is a figure in some of those pictures who appears somewhat sombre. In one picture, in which guests at several tables have turned to face the photographer, she can be seen in the background looking like she'd rather be anywhere else. She's dressed immaculately, in keeping with the day, but her expression is completely at odds with everybody else's. It's as if perhaps she doesn't approve of the blessing that has taken place, or is somehow wise to trouble ahead.

Her name was Irene Bomford, and I had just become her daughter-in-law.

16
Irene

'*Now, Mrs Bomford*'. *My father with mother-in-law Irene on our wedding day.*

Our honeymoon was wonderful. We went to Scotland for a week. It rained constantly, but nothing could dampen my sense that I had married the right man. As every day passed, however, I felt a looming unease about my return. I had made my decision to leave Quarry Pits, and wanted to be with Tony without question. What didn't sit comfortably with me was where we would begin our lives together.

'We'll be completely independent,' Tony had said, when he first raised the prospect of moving in with his parents at their farmhouse near South Littleton. 'As well as a bedroom we'll have our own kitchen. I've just helped to convert the old dairy, and made it cosy but comfortable. Joan, it'll be like having a place all to ourselves!'

He had made it sound quite wonderful, and his enthusiasm won me over. Tony's family farmhouse was certainly an attractive place to live. Norval, as it was called, offered plenty of space and yet I struggled to look forward to the day that we moved in. For one thing, it was some ride from Quarry Pits on the bicycle, but that wasn't uppermost on my mind as we drove back to Worcestershire. Sure enough, just as soon as Tony and I pulled up outside Norval as newlyweds, the welcome we received from his mother did little to ease my misgivings.

'I'll show you to your room,' she said from the door, as if perhaps we had just arrived at board and lodgings and would be expected to be on our way the next day.

Physically, Irene Bomford was small in stature. Like me, she made up for that in other ways. Even so, we couldn't have been more different. While I had been raised to muck in and help out wherever possible, Irene preferred it if the people around her just fell into line. She liked everything to be done in her own way, and made it very clear when she didn't approve of something. It made this little lady much larger than life in a formidable way.

Very quickly, I learned that Irene did not approve of me.

I tried hard not to take it personally, but that was tough when we lived under the same roof. Every single thing I did and every word I spoke was met by a reproachful look. When I expressed a desire to bring my dear old pony, Sparks, to live up on the farm's stable, it was ruled out without a word directed at me. Even being in Irene's presence would leave me feeling as if the temperature had just dropped by a degree, and so I did my best to steer clear. Instead, I decided to play to my strengths, and took to helping Tony's father around his farm. A lovely man, both witty and wise, Trevor quickly came to appreciate the fact that I could drive a tractor or turn the hay like any of his men. But even when he sang my praises back at the farmhouse, Irene just pretended not to hear. If anything, it just placed our relationship under even greater strain.

'She lives for her son,' Trevor said to me one day while we were herding cows. 'Your new husband is the apple of her eye, and always will be. Doesn't matter how happy you make him, the fact is you've taken him away from her.'

'So what can I do?' I asked, but Trevor just shrugged.

'She'll come round,' he said. 'I dare say it'll take a while, but you'll prove yourself to her in time.'

It was a relief, in some ways, to hear that I wasn't doing anything wrong. At the same time, I had to get used to the fact that I couldn't do anything right. I began to expect Irene's criticism, usually delivered indirectly, and though I considered myself to be hardy it soon dented my confidence. Once, having washed our laundry in a bath tub outside, because she wouldn't permit me to use the big sink in her kitchen, I hung the clothes on the line before retreating to our bedroom. I'd had to boil a kettle several times for hot water, and then worked up a lather knowing full well that she was watching me from inside. It was an uncomfortable experience, and as soon I reached our room I shut the door feeling relieved to be free from her gaze. A moment later, on hearing activity outside, I crossed to peek from the window.

Down in the courtyard, I saw my mother-in-law inspecting the clothes I had hung out to dry. She pinched each garment between her fingers, and I wondered what on earth she was doing. Then, much to my horror and amazement, she unpegged everything, dropped it into the basket and carried it all inside.

A little later that day, the laundry reappeared on the line. It had been washed a second time, using Irene's preferred choice of detergent.

'She means well,' said Tony, when I told him what had happened, though it was clear to me that he felt as awkward about it as I was upset.

'She's making her opinion of me quite plain,' I insisted. 'My washing doesn't come up to her standards, and neither do I. I'm not good enough for you, Tony! That's what she's trying to say!'

For a moment, my new husband looked torn.

'I know she can be difficult,' he said.

'And it's making life intolerable!'

Tony drew breath to respond, paused as if to consider what he was about to say, and then let the air from his lungs in a long sigh.

'She's considering giving us a plot of land over in the next field,' he said finally. 'It's nothing much. Just enough to build on when we can afford a place of our own.'

'And that would make things better now?' I looked up at Tony squarely, in no mood to feel as if I should be grateful after the way she had treated me.

'Whatever happens,' he said finally, coming to sit beside me on the bed, 'we're in this together. We'll work it out, Joan. I promise you.'

I had to believe that Tony was right, for throughout those early days I would visit Quarry Pits and realise just how miserable my life had become. My parents couldn't believe what Irene had done with my washing, but shared my father-in-law's opinion that she couldn't maintain such animosity when I was plainly a decent soul.

'I have no doubt you'll win her over,' said Mother. 'All you can do is be true to yourself.'

It was Tony's aunt, Hilda, who came up with a novel solution to the laundry humiliation that Irene continued to put me through. Every time I laboured over the washing in the yard, and hung it up to dry, within minutes it would be gone for what she considered to be a thorough scrub.

'Don't waste your time if Irene's just going to do it all again,' said Hilda, who knew full well what her sister could be like. 'Just hang up your dirty clothes!'

Her advice made me laugh out loud. It was a rare moment for me at that time, but I decided to take her advice. As I couldn't find a way to talk to Irene, and even her own son had tried and failed, it felt like a way of sending back a response at last.

And so, the next time I had a bundle of dirty washing, I carried it through the kitchen in a basket. But instead of putting the kettle on to begin the tortuous process of filling the tub in the yard, I simply headed outside and began to hang each shirt and sock on the line. I no longer cared about the promise of a scrap of land. I wasn't going to allow her to hold me to ransom over that. Well, Irene pretended not to notice when I came back inside, of course, but I knew she had seen me. I also felt sure that she couldn't bear the thought of all those grubby garments dangling from her line.

Within minutes, our dry, unwashed clothes had vanished from the line. Sometime later, they reappeared all pegged up neatly having been scrubbed and wrung through.

From that day onwards, whenever I did our laundry, I hung it out on the line safe in the knowledge that Irene would leave it to dry. Nothing more was ever mentioned about that episode, but it was the first time, perhaps, that Irene Bomford realised that I was a force to be reckoned with.

A short while afterwards, we learned through Tony's father that she had finally decided to grant us a plot of land we could call our own. He had been waiting to gift it to us for some time, but it had taken this long for Irene to come round. When Tony broke the news, beaming at me with both hands spread wide, I responded by turning to the window. The farmhouse overlooked the field in question; a broad expanse of lowland meadow defined by wild hedgerow. We would, in effect, be immediate neighbours.

'You see the field just beyond,' I said to Tony, and waited for him to nod. 'The plot would be better there.'

'Why?' Tony looked puzzled. 'That's right on the edge of Norval's farm land.'

'Exactly!' I said, and grinned at him. 'As far from here as possible, and out of eyeshot, too,' I added, mindful of the hedgerow between the two fields.

Tony thought about this for a moment, and then his expression brightened.

'So we can't be overlooked?' he said, and began to nod as if answering his own question. 'I'll have a word with Dad. No doubt he'll understand.'

It was a small concession, and I was mindful to thank Trevor for being so understanding when he agreed that we could build at the back of the far field. Despite her blessing, my mother-in-law remained resolute in her belief that somehow her son could've done better. At the same time, I learned to pick my battles. Had I gone head to head with Irene over everything, no doubt I would've lost. Instead, I learned to complete my chores in the household before heading across to the plot of land that I hoped to turn into a home one day.

I didn't go to stand and daydream. I went to scout the surrounding area in search of fields to farm. If we were going to build a house, I believed that it could be done from the proceeds of crops or livestock. With meadowland stretching far beyond the boundary of Norval, I felt as if luck had looked kindly upon me when I found eight acres of neglected market garden, just a stone's throw from our plot. It belonged to a neighbouring farmer who had grown too frail to tend to his vegetables, and so I made him an offer. It might've been money we had set aside in savings, but this struck me as an investment that would go beyond the build.

With Tony, I restored that 'Man's Land' of a market garden into a fertile oasis of vegetable crops. By saving a few pennies, we also bought a paving slab each week and began to lay a path from the lane to our little plot. Within a couple of months, we could walk there in good shoes.

Throughout this time, whenever the atmosphere seriously soured up at Norval, I would head back to visit Quarry Pits. By then, John was beginning to work alongside Dad on an equal basis. Father had only just turned sixty, and though he knew that one day Brother would take over completely they sometimes pushed and pulled over what was best for the farm. I would often hear both sides, but they always worked things out cordially. I enjoyed spending time with

Mother, too, while Marian worked tirelessly to support her. Then there was Sparks. Even though I'd moved out, she remained my responsibility and I loved spending time with her. If I'd felt the need to get away from Irene, it came as a comfort to be able to ride out and just forget about the situation for a while.

Tony knew how much that little old piebald meant to me. He was also well aware that mother-in-law Irene considered her to be a scrappy nag that needed putting down. With no possibility of using the stable up at Norval, he proposed that we build a little shed for Sparks at the back of our field and stable her there.

'What about your mother?' I asked, for even just considering how she would respond had taken the shine off his proposal.

'It's our land,' said Tony, as if perhaps I had forgotten.

And that's how the pony from my childhood followed me into my adult life. I would tend to her regularly, and even bring her grass as there was nowhere for her to graze. The shed was very basic, but we rode out every day. In fact, I saw more of her there than ever before. With Tony helping his father, who welcomed me working alongside them, things were beginning to look up. Even if I still had a long way to go before my mother-in-law accepted me, my new world was starting to feel a little bit brighter.

It was Tony's father, however, who enabled it to shine.

'Old Sparks looks like she could use some company,' said Trevor one day, having paid a visit to our market garden while we were harvesting our crop by hand. Right from the start, when I first assessed that plot and ploughed the soil, he had expressed his admiration at the way I managed it. Just then, in front of her stall, Trevor watched us at work while Sparks nuzzled him in a bid for attention. 'How is she with cattle?' he asked me next.

'Fine.' I stopped to wipe my brow, puzzled by his question. 'I think.'

'Then maybe she'd like to spend some time up at the top field,' he suggested. 'You can leave her up there to graze every day.'

He was talking about the field adjoining the farmhouse, where he often kept his cows.

'Won't that be a problem?' I asked, without mentioning Irene by name.

My father-in-law shrugged.

'Let's face it,' he said, and gestured at my pony with the brown and white patches. 'Surrounded by a herd, she could be mistaken for a Friesian.'

I looked at Sparks and then laughed out loud, just as Tony crossed the field to join us.

'Have I missed something?' he asked, looking both amused and puzzled when I relayed the invitation.

'I was just saying how your mother never notices when we buy a new cow at market,' his father said, and gestured towards Sparks.

Tony chuckled, and then winked at me.

'If Dad says it's okay then I'm sure she'll blend right in,' he agreed. 'Though we'll have to watch out for her at milking.'

It took a very long time before Irene Bomford rumbled us. Even when she finally registered the horse that grazed among the herd, she didn't complain about it directly. By then, so much had come between us that it must've seemed insignificant.

17

A Test of Motherhood

Tony and I on an evening out.

In the spring of 1955, I learned that I was pregnant with our first child.

Tony was overjoyed. A grin broke out across his face, which set that way for days. My mother-in-law shared in his delight. Like her husband, Trevor, she was genuinely thrilled at the prospect of becoming a grandparent. I felt a great sense of relief. Although I didn't slow down throughout my pregnancy, and carried on working the whole time, it was a happy time.

Of course, in the last month or so the bump got in the way, and I began to feel quite tired. Even so, I wasn't going to let that stop me from pulling my weight around the farm. Not only did I have my chores in the farmhouse, Tony and his dad had come to rely on my help with the cows at milking time. Above all, I had designs for our little market garden. I was determined to use those eight acres as a seedbed for our new life, and so I barely rested.

Joanne Marie Bomford arrived in late November, and immediately went by her middle name only. She was born in hospital, where Tony drove me in haste after I had gone into labour at the farm-house. I had been to market that day as well, and only just put my feet up when I realised the time had come. Little Marie was a breech birth, and I stayed on the maternity ward with her for several weeks. That's just how it was in those days. I was so pleased when they discharged us, and shared in Tony's pride when he drove us home to Norval. There, I carried our little bundle over the threshold into the farmhouse, and immediately faced my first test of motherhood.

'So, you're back.'

Irene stood at the door to her kitchen with her arms folded. It was my father-in-law who had greeted us at the door, pumping Tony's hand, hugging me and cooing over Marie. It was a lovely moment, just as it should've been, but it was spoiled by Irene's welcome. One look at her expression reminded me of how she had been before my pregnancy: that mouth drawn tight as if pulled by purse strings and a gaze that defied you to meet her eye.

'Would you like to hold her?' I offered. 'She's good as gold.'

My instinct was to cradle Marie protectively. Even with Tony's hand on my shoulder, I felt vulnerable, and yet I knew that I had to give Irene this chance.

'Go on, Mum,' said Tony. 'See how it feels to be a granny!'

I stepped forward, with my attention locked on the baby but my thoughts focused entirely on my mother-in-law. She made no effort to step forward or take Marie until I got so close that she had no choice.

'Very well,' she said, as if I had just asked her to hold a sack of potatoes.

I stood back, feeling strikingly bereft. It was a feeling made all the more uncomfortable as Irene appraised the new-born in her arms. Marie was asleep, unaware of her grandmother's cold, hard gaze. As I waited for her to say something, the sound of Tony and his father chatting trailed away. A moment later, my mother-in-law offered the barest hint of a smile. Then she handed Marie back to me, and I realised that smile had been for nobody else but herself.

'Isn't she lovely?' said Trevor, but Irene didn't seem to register him.

Instead, with the baby restored to my arms, she waited until she had my full attention.

'You ought to have drowned her in a pool,' she said calmly, before turning her back and returning to her kitchen.

I had delivered a grandchild to my mother-in-law, and failed her. That's how Irene saw things. Had Tony and I returned with a baby boy, things would've been different. In her eyes, what this farming dynasty needed was a son to follow in Tony's footsteps.

'She doesn't mean it,' he assured me, but this time I was not to be placated.

'How can anyone say such a thing?' I asked him through my tears. I was also very angry. Upstairs in our room, rocking Marie who had awoken for her feed, I sought to console myself as much as the baby.

'Give her time,' he asked.

'She doesn't deserve it,' I said. 'Not after that.'

'Joan, we have to try to get along,' he said. 'This is her house, remember.'

I took Marie to the window. I couldn't see our plot of land across the fields on account of the hedgerow, but I knew it was out there.

'I'll do my best,' I said, and faced him once more. 'But we can't live here forever. It isn't fair to us, but more importantly it isn't fair to our little girl.'

Tony listened to what I had to say and I knew that I had his support. It must've been tough for him to see the mother he loved behaving in such an appalling way. He had just witnessed her effectively reject his first-born, and yet as he embraced us both I felt quite sure that we would see this through as a family.

With Christmas fast approaching, I was determined to make it a memorable event. Even living under Irene's reproachful eye, I wanted to enjoy the occasion with my husband and our new child. I decided that it would be nice to roast a goose, and selected a plump one for the table. Perhaps my ambitions got the better of me, however, because once I'd prepared the bird in our dairy kitchen I discovered that it wouldn't fit inside the oven. Tony's father had kindly given us an electric Baby Belling model. It was only little. With the goose squeezed three-quarters of the way inside, I had to tie shut the oven door with string. It meant I needed to turn it several times, and give it an extra hour to be sure it was cooked through, but I got there in the end.

'Delicious!' declared Tony, on tucking in. I had even prepared a little plate for Marie, and mashed it up with gravy so she could manage it. Dabbing his mouth, Tony invited me to look around. We were eating at a little table in our dairy kitchen, away from Irene who hadn't invited us to dine with them. Frost coated the outside of the window looking out onto the courtyard, but my husband was happy and so was I. 'This is where it all begins, Joan,' he said, and raised a glass as a toast. 'Here's to happy families!'

We weren't to know that Marie was allergic to goose meat, but it was clear to us both within the hour. Her face, chest and neck broke out in hives, and she cried throughout the rest of the day. We took turns in pacing the house with her, doing everything we could to make her feel more comfortable. When Irene asked me why she wouldn't stop crying, and I explained what had happened, her response just made me feel guiltier.

'A fit and proper mother wouldn't make that mistake,' she said, without offering to take the baby, which persuaded me to take Marie to our bedroom where I could soothe her in peace.

As the New Year dawned, it came as no surprise to anyone when I took up my duties around the farm once more. Baby Marie and I hadn't been home for long. She took up a great deal of my time, as any young mother will know, and yet I couldn't just sit in a nursing chair and rest. Within a short space of time, I was back out in the farm, helping with the herd.

'She'll be mooing before she says her first word,' joked Trevor, when I showed up for milking with my daughter in tow. Tony and I had bought a pram for her. It was a huge old thing with a retractable hood and wheels that looked better suited to a bicycle. Having wrapped our daughter against the cold I took to trundling her out in that thing so she could watch me work. It also gave me breathing space from Irene, which was something both Tony and his father appreciated that I needed so desperately. And when we'd finished filling the milk churns, I'd push Marie out down the lane to our market garden.

Very quickly, those eight acres became a refuge to me. There wasn't much to be done in those colder months, but I would go there to plan and size up the surrounding land. When I heard that an elderly, neighbouring farmer was set to give up on his pigs, I wheeled Marie across to see him and offered to take the swine off his hands along with the land they were on. I couldn't offer much. Tony had been saving what he could from his wages, and I had some money set aside from the sale of the last cow my dad had given to me, but it proved to be enough. As a result, our market garden expanded to embrace a muddy plot behind it with several squealing porkers and a Nissen hut for a sty. The extra work in taking care of it all meant Marie spent the remains of that winter and much of the spring in the open air. It could be chilly sometimes, but I took good care of her. Despite it all, nothing could compare to how cold things became at the farmhouse.

'She's crying again,' Irene took to complaining whenever my back was turned.

For a baby who seemed so content whenever we were tending to the cows, the pigs and the market garden, Marie just seemed so unsettled around her grandmother. Throughout the rest of that year,

I would leave them for a moment and an infant wail would draw me back.

'I'm sorry,' I would say whenever Irene had lifted the baby to soothe her. By then, she had taken to holding Marie every now and then, but did so as if to suggest that someone had to look after her properly.

'You haven't fed her goose meat again, have you?' she asked once.

'Of course not.' I took my daughter so I could calm her. 'I give her everything she needs, but then sometimes this happens.'

'Perhaps she just hasn't bonded with you,' she said, before leaving me to think about it. 'It happens to some mothers.'

Trevor Bomford was a loyal husband to Irene, but even he had limits. She could tell him what to do and he would do so without question, but he also had time for me.

'Next time you leave Marie with Irene,' he said once. 'You'd be minded to have eyes in the back of your head.'

I asked him what he meant by this, but we were milking at the time and could only think he hadn't heard me on account of the noise. I took his advice though, out of curiosity as much as a sense of suspicion, and discovered a side to my mother-in-law that proved so shocking that I knew we had to leave.

'She pinches Marie awake!' I told Tony just as soon as we were alone together, and then shared what I had witnessed earlier that day. 'I left the room when the baby was fast asleep and crept back to the door to watch.'

'Are you quite sure?' Tony looked deeply troubled.

'Irene crossed to the pram just as soon as I left and she nipped her on the arm! I couldn't believe it, Tony, but it's true. She just wants to make me feel miserable, but I'm not standing for it any longer. We have to leave.'

'And go where?'

I drew his attention to the window.

'It's time to build a place of our own.'

'But we don't have enough money,' he reasoned. 'We need to keep saving.'

'We can get a mortgage,' I told him. 'I've done the sums. A thousand pounds will do it.'

Tony gazed through the window, deep in thought.

'If we wait another year I'll have the money to commission a builder outright.'

'It can't wait!' I said so forcefully that he turned to face me. I took his hands and looked up into his eyes. 'I'm pregnant again.'

PART THREE

18

A Herd and a Home

At a country show aged nineteen.

I grew up watching crops rise from the soil. My dad taught me how to plough the land, plant out and then let nature take its course across a season. In 1957, I witnessed something very different take shape from the ground. As the sun strengthened and the days grew longer, a home came into existence; wrought from brick, timber and slate.

As soon as Tony learned that we were expecting our second child, he worked so hard to provide us with a place of our own. Straight away, we went to see a local builder called Ted Newbold. He was chairman of our Young Farmers club, and we knew him well. He also understood why we needed to leave Norval as soon as possible.

'I can build that for you,' he said, when we took him to the plot and shared our vision. It was a modest proposal. We had decided that a little bungalow would suit us just fine. Tony shared my belief that we had no need for anything fancy. With the market garden and the pigs, and my watchful eye for any adjacent land that we might put to good use, most of our time was spent outside.

'How long will it take?' Tony patted my growing bump. 'We have a deadline.'

Ted Newbold pondered the plot of rough grassland. In his mind's eye, I imagined he could see the building that would come to be our family home.

'Well, the petrol rationing will be an issue,' he told us, which caused my heart to sink a little. Even a decade after the war had come to an end, we were still living with the consequences. The fuel limitations affected everyone.

'So, what do you estimate?' asked Tony. He exchanged an anxious look with me. 'Six months?'

Ted scoffed at this, turning to face us at the same time.

'I can't afford to pay my men to travel out here every day for that length of time!' he declared.

By now, I had resigned myself to living under my mother-in-law's shadow for the foreseeable future. I felt like a prisoner who had been given a glimpse of freedom, only to have that taken away from her. Then Ted caught my eye and winked at me.

'Don't look so worried, Joan,' he said. 'The only way I can make this pay is by transporting all my men here every day in one truck. Providing they put their backs into it, and they will if they want to get paid, I can have it completed for you in a month.'

From our bedroom at Norval, it took no more than a week before I could see the beginning of our home peep over the hedgerow.

It was an exciting time. Not only did I have a beautiful baby, who was good as gold for me, but another one was on the way. Together with Tony, I could see myself making a home for us all in the bungalow before the roof joists were locked into place. Every day, I would finish the milking and help to swill down the cattle shed, before taking Marie down to the plot to check on progress.

I could see the workmen from the lane. They looked like ants, crawling over the shell of the building, which began to look adrift in a lake of mud, but I didn't mind that one bit. Surrounded by open fields, defined by elm trees and wild hedgerow, I felt like we were soon to be taking up residence in our own private paradise. Between us, in recognition of the support that Trevor had given us, as well as Irene's granting us the land, we decided to name our new place after the cow herd bred and raised at Norval.

'Moyfield,' said Tony, trying it out for size. 'Sounds like my kind of home.'

With building progressing so rapidly, my thoughts turned to how we would furnish the bungalow. All our savings had been committed to the mortgage, the upkeep of the market garden and the pigs. We just couldn't afford to go out and buy things brand new, and so I started to look out for old items that might find a second life in our home. My parents were very good to us, and helped us with a bed to sleep on, and table and chairs to eat our meals, while a trip I made to cattle market one day saw me return with an unexpected item of furniture.

'Excuse me, Sir,' I said to the market drover, after cleaning out the back of Trevor's truck. 'What is that?'

I was standing with the man in front of a steaming muck heap. What had grabbed my attention was a wooden carving. It was only partially visible at the back, but I couldn't mistake the lion's head.

'That,' he said, 'is a crying shame.'

I asked him what he meant. In response, the drover took a fork from the heap and cleared the muck around the carving so I could see.

'Is it a dresser?' I asked when it became visible to me. By now, I realised that I had glimpsed just a mounting atop a sizeable piece of furniture.

'It's been propped at the back there for ages,' he said, 'but it would look lovely all cleaned up.'

I glanced behind me. The back of the cattle truck that I had just swept out was empty. With help, I could fit it in there.

'How much do you want for it?' I asked, before returning home a pound lighter but with a truck that was possibly heavier than when I had set out with two Friesians on board.

Tony looked at me like I had gone mad when I reversed the truck towards the bungalow. The builders had helped to create an access drive from the lane where we first laid out the paving slabs. From my wing mirror, I spotted some of them approaching down it to see what I had brought for them.

'What on earth is it?' my husband asked when I lowered the tailgate.

'A work of art,' I said from the back of the truck, and rested my hands on my waist. 'After a good scrub, it's going to take pride of place in our front room.'

Amid much chuckling from the builders, Tony turned to size up the building site.

'It'll never fit through the front door,' he said.

'Then it's lucky the front door hasn't been fitted yet!' I laughed, for this was something I had already considered.

Tony returned his attention to the back of the vehicle. Already, some of the builders had volunteered to help me unload. With a sigh, and a chuckle, he stepped up to assist them.

'You know what I love about you, Joan?' he said. 'You're a woman with vision. You see the potential in something, even if nobody else does, and you make it shine.'

The Gargoyle, as I came to call it, turned out to be a Victorian court cupboard. Built from solid oak, it still stands resplendent in the front room. There's no way we could get it out again now, and I love it. I restored it to the best of my abilities, and I'm told that it could be worth a lot of money, but it isn't for sale. In some ways, it reminds me of Tony's assessment of the way I like to do things, as became apparent in the years that followed. With the bungalow complete, I could've settled into a life devoted to motherhood while my husband assisted his father on the dairy farm. Instead, as well as my designs for expanding the market garden, I began to think that I could use the surrounding land for a long-standing passion of mine. What's more, I hoped that it would also bring out the best in people who hadn't been so blessed in life as me.

But first I had a second baby to bring into the world.

Out first son was born in the September of that year, and named after his two lovely grandfathers. To avoid confusion with the one we saw every day from Norval, everyone called Trevor Anthony Colin Bomford by his last name, and the arrangement just stuck. My dad was thrilled, not just because his grandson would come to answer to the same name as him, but by the fact that he was so strong and healthy. He and Mother might've been some distance away, and busy with the farm at Quarry Pits, but they drove over regularly to see us all, and even took care of Marie in the first weeks of her brother's life to ease the strain on us. She really was the apple of my dad's eye. On the day they brought our daughter home, and said hello for the first time to their new grandson, she toddled out when nobody was looking and took it upon herself to paint his beloved Wolseley with creosote. Fortunately, we managed to scrub it off before it dried, and Father never had a cross word to say about it.

Little Colin was a bundle of joy. He had a lusty pair of lungs on him, and a birthmark on his ankle that Tony said looked just like the face of a fox. Having raised Marie, I felt confident in the way I cared for him, and we bonded quickly. Once again, I returned to working with Trevor and Tony as soon as I could, and put the big old pram to good use for a second time. It was a lovely time, working alongside two generations of Bomford boys with a third one swaddled soundly in my care and his big sister playing nearby. But it was Irene who made life just a little bit easier for me.

This time, on presenting her with the grandson she had hoped for the first time round, her manner softened considerably.

'He's a handsome chap,' she said, rocking the baby in her arms. 'Takes after his father.'

I chose to say nothing. By then, even if she said anything barbed I simply chose to ignore it. As soon as we moved from Norval, I no longer felt as if my mother-in-law commanded such power over me. She was still a formidable woman, but I could walk away from her now.

'We should be getting on,' I said, once she'd handed the baby back to me. 'We need to see a man about some chickens.'

Irene frowned, as I had anticipated, and so I busied myself making sure her grandson was comfortable in the pram. As well as maintaining the farmhouse, Irene took care of the poultry at Norval as well as the pigs. I suppose I could've asked her for some chicks – I had designs on starting my own flock – but I knew from bitter experience that she would've found a way to hold that over me.

'Where will you put them?' she asked. 'You can say goodbye to your market garden if you're thinking of keeping them with your crops.'

I smiled politely, wondering if she was being entirely serious. Having grown up with a mother who maintained a flock of several thousand, I knew full well what chickens could do if let loose in the broccoli and asparagus. I was no fool, even if it had felt like Irene took me for one from the day her son asked for my hand in marriage.

'A little plot of land has come up for sale over at the back of ours,' I said. 'Properly fenced, I plan to keep enough hens to turn a profit on the eggs.'

Irene snorted dismissively.

'You'll hardly make a fortune, Girl. And you want to be careful throwing away Tony's money like that. I dare say there are more fruitful ventures.'

'I dare say you're right,' I said, with both hands grasping the pram handles. Irene was wearing that expression that demanded servitude, I refused to bow to it, and looked right back at her. 'In fact,'

I continued, 'every penny we make from the eggs, along with the sale of our crops and the pigs at market, will go towards something else I have in mind. We've a long way to go, but I'm going to make it happen.'

'And what is that?' Irene seemed taken aback by the note of defiance in my voice.

My baby stirred in the pram just then; awoken by the hardening in his grandmother's voice, perhaps. I took a breath, refusing to look away.

'A riding school,' I said after a moment.

Irene's nostrils flared. She folded her arms and appeared to grow in stature at the same time.

'Does Tony know about this?' she asked, as if her son would surely put a stop to such nonsense.

'He's right behind me every step of the way,' I was delighted to confirm.

19

About the Car

On Lil-Sarah. I have always had a love of horses.

It was Nimrod – the cow which had served me so well as a little girl in the absence of a horse – that kindled my interest in teaching people how to ride. My brother John first climbed into the saddle with my encouragement, and took the reins as I instructed. Even though Nimrod grew tired of our efforts, and turned her attention to the bull, I never forgot the sense of pride and satisfaction that comes from watching a novice rider place their trust in me.

In my last years at Quarry Pits, I found that riding Sparks often drew local children to ask if I would tutor them. I gladly obliged, charging two shillings an hour, and enjoyed the experience as much as those who learned to ride. But it wasn't until we'd moved into the bungalow, bringing Sparks back so she could be with me, that I considered it as a possible business venture. In fact, Tony and I had barely settled in when two girls knocked upon my door.

'Will you teach us?' they asked, and revealed the coins in their palms.

Their names were Gina and Barbara; two earnest little things who looked at my pony in awe and wonder when I led them out to the patch of land where I kept her.

'He can be a handful,' I warned. 'Sparks by name, and sparky by nature.'

Gina and Barbara looked totally unfazed. They had their parents' blessing, they assured me and so I took them out onto the drive for their very first lesson.

With so much to do in tending to the market garden, raising pigs and my new flock of chickens, not to mention two young children, it was a challenge to find the time. Even so, with regular visits, those little girls learned how to ride, trot and canter on Sparks, and left with a newfound confidence. That's when I knew for sure what I wanted to do, and Tony gave me his full blessing on one condition.

'You'll need insurance,' he said. 'Riders regularly fall off, and it's our responsibility to make sure everything is done properly.'

'Insurance is expensive,' I pointed out, but Tony insisted.

If I was going to make it happen, I knew that I would have to devote myself to saving up.

In those early years at the bungalow, I made sure every spare penny went into my war chest. The poultry proved to be a great success. I sold eggs from the end of the drive and at market, and also established a reputation for providing quality chicken for the table. When Tony built a garage, I used the space at the side to breed rabbits, for there was still a demand in kitchens across the region. It was hard work, especially with my daily duties with the cattle at Norval, but my savings for the riding school began to grow – and so too did our family.

In February 1961, little Joe came into the world. He was born on my bed at the bungalow, having given me no warning that he was on the way. I had been mending a fence when I felt him coming, and only just managed to raise Tony in time. In contrast to his dramatic arrival, Joe was such a happy-go-lucky little chap. Always smiling, he was adored by his older siblings and fitted easily into life at the bungalow. With support from my parents, who doted on their grandchildren, I was able to continue working hard, and the day grew closer when I could turn my dream into a reality.

By then, I had taken out cover to teach children on Sparks, and when a small waiting list of children began to form I even bought another pony. If Sparks was lively, Roly was plain naughty. He'd happily walk with a little rider in the saddle, only to drop down, unseat the poor thing and enjoy a good roll in the dirt. As model riding-school ponies they were hopeless, but both made up for it with bags of character. Most importantly of all, the children who came to me adored them.

I look upon that time with great affection. Tony and I were setting down roots. Our three children were finding their voices and also their feet, we'd bought a jeep to get out and about, while our rural patch of paradise continued to expand and thrive. As is often the case, however, it took an unexpected event to remind me that life should never be taken for granted.

In 1962 Colin Collins, my beloved father, suffered a stroke. For a farmer, it was a catastrophic setback. Although he recovered sufficiently to walk and talk, and could take the wheel of a tractor, he was obliged to hand over the bulk of his responsibilities to John. Like me, Brother was very close to our dad. John did everything he could to involve him in the fields at Quarry Pits, but it would never be the same again. It wasn't just Father's stroke that changed things. The agricultural demand for steam-powered engines was beginning to dwindle, and diesel and petrol-driven tractors were now commonplace in the fields, while combine harvesters threatened the future of our threshing machines. Over the decades, in a bid to keep up with demand from farms in need of his services, Father had amassed four steam engines in total. Once, there had been a time when the machines were contracted out so frequently they were rarely seen at Quarry Pits. Now, they often sat idle at the side of the rick yard; in danger of falling prey to rust and becoming entangled with weeds.

'We had to sell one,' John told me when I paid him a visit. He had come out to meet me, wiping his hands on an oily rag. My brother looked troubled, I noted, and addressed me as if perhaps I could help. 'Dad doesn't like to talk about it,' he went on, 'but I had no choice. We have wages to pay, Joan. Our men look to us to put food on the table.'

'You've done the right thing,' I assured him, before heading inside to see Father.

Since his stroke, I had taken it upon myself to drop in as much as possible. As Marie was old enough to talk, and report on any funny business, I felt comfortable leaving the children with Irene. She could still be caustic at times, but the presence of two grandsons brought out a kinder side that she displayed towards all three of them.

'So, you know,' said my dad, when I found him in his office. I could only think he must've seen me talking to John from a window, though I was mindful of John's advice. It felt strange to find him doing paperwork during daylight hours, but Mother insisted that he put his health first. He still looked as strong as an ox, with his broad face and shoulders supporting thick braces, but that spark in his manner had dimmed considerably. It struck me that every move he made seemed to require some thought. Even rising from his chair to greet me was a struggle for him.

'That engine served you well,' I said, 'but it's important to move with the times.'

Dad looked unconvinced. His attention turned to the doorway just then. I looked around to see Mother.

'It's upset him quite a bit,' she said.

'I'm not upset,' he insisted, but neither of us took him to task. 'How are the little ones?' he asked, if only to break the silence that followed, and gripped the edge of his desk as he lowered himself into his seat once more.

'One of the horses nibbled Joe on the toe,' I said, which caused him to chuckle. As Mother went off to make a pot of tea, I settled in the chair opposite and told him how I'd left the baby in his pram, sleeping by the stock fence overlooking the horse paddock, and then rushed out to him on hearing him wail. Dad smiled when I assured him there was no harm done, and then asked after Joe's brother and sister in turn. As we talked, a light came into those tired, weakened eyes like the glow from a firebox. Father was so proud of his grandchildren, as he was of his own offspring, and, of course, of all that he had achieved with Kitty. Even so, I returned home that afternoon with a sense of melancholy I could not shake off.

The telephone call, when it came several months later, still served to draw my breath in a gasp.

'He's dying,' my sister, Marian, said. 'Come quickly.'

It took me several minutes to gather my wits. I was in shock, and not sure what to do. As Tony and his father were away for the day, having taken our jeep, my guiding instinct led me to gather the children and hurry across to Norval. I knew that Irene would be at home at that time, and would be sure to help me in an emergency.

'Can I borrow your car?' I asked breathlessly, with Joe in my arms and the other two at my side.

'Whatever for?' She was taken aback by the urgency in my manner, and stepped aside so that Marie and Colin could file into the farmhouse. When I told her why I needed to get to Quarry Pits, I assumed she would fetch me the key straight away. Instead, she considered my request as if I had just affronted her.

'No,' she said finally. 'You may not.'

For a second, I stood there in stunned silence. I felt a surge of anger, but knew well enough not to give her the satisfaction of expressing it. Instead, with no time to stand on her doorstep and argue, and mindful that Marian had told me the end was close, I thrust Joe into Irene's arms and rushed to collect Tony's bicycle from the yard.

'Joan!' she called after me, but I did not stop to give her a second more.

As the crow flies, across river meadow and woodland, Inkberrow is just eight miles from South Littleton. By road, it's nearly double the distance. By car, I could've been there in no time. Instead, pedalling as fast as I could, even when my legs screamed at me to stop as I struggled with the hills, it took me close to an hour. On reaching Quarry Pits, I dropped the bike at the foot of the slope and crashed through the kitchen door. There, panting hard, I stopped in my tracks.

'I'm sorry,' said John, who had broken from the gathering around the bedside upstairs, where Colin Collins lay still.

'When?' I asked, and choked back tears as I fought for breath.

From somewhere in the farmhouse, I could hear the sound of weeping.

'A few minutes ago.' My brother bowed his head. 'He was quite at peace.'

Father passed away aged sixty-eight. It wasn't old for a man of the soil who had lived to plough, plant and harvest, and we mourned him. At his funeral, up at the church in Dormston, so many people came to pay their respects from across the village and beyond. He had made one hundred acres of land his own, and yet his wisdom, kindness and indefatigable spirit reached far and wide. Just after we laid him to rest in the little graveyard, and drifted towards the church gate, I sensed a presence beside me. I turned to see Irene. Despite the veil, I could see her looking at me with trepidation.

'I'm sorry about the car,' she said quietly. 'It was wrong of me.'

I nodded, still walking with her.

'Thank you,' I said.

And then she stopped me. She reached out with her hand, clasped my elbow and that brought me to a halt.

'I've been wrong about you, too,' she said, and nodded to herself as if to gather confidence. 'You're a good wife, a good mother and a good daughter, too. I judged you badly, Joan, and I hope someday you can forgive me.'

20

Trespassers

A home of our own.

Like so many people in grief, my work became a source of comfort to me. I couldn't just take time off from the milking or the market garden, while the pigs, the chickens and the rabbits required daily care. In a sense, farming can serve as a great leveller. It reminds you that life goes on from one season to the next.

Losing my dad made me all the more determined to pursue my dream. Naturally, I had sought his advice about my plans to establish a riding school. Even though he'd gone, I still carried his encouragement with me. Every day, I'd wake on the cusp of dawn and consider ways to bring in more money so that I could make it happen. Farmers often traded land with each other, and so I turned my attention to the fields beyond our bungalow. I would be first, I resolved, to make an offer whenever a local farmer or grower put land up for sale or rent.

Slowly, over the course of several years, our holding continued to increase in size. We took on pasture near the village, complete with a cowshed, which Tony populated with cattle, and when a sizeable acreage across the lane came up for sale at auction I kept my hand raised until the hammer came down. Every time, our savings dwindled and then swelled again when our livestock began to provide a return. It was a long and challenging process, but I never once lost faith. In fact, when times were tough, and sometimes it seemed unending, both Tony and I left the fields at sundown to take on work in town. We'd pack the children into the car and head for the Park View Hotel in Evesham. There, Tony would wash up in the kitchens while I served tables as a waitress. As for Marie, Colin and Joe, they were taken under the wing of the chefs, porters and dining-room staff, and spoiled rotten. By the time we returned to the bungalow at the end of each shift, all of us were exhausted. Despite it all I would be up at first light and another day closer to achieving my dream of running a fully-fledged riding school.

Around that time, I even found extra work in the saddle. John Jordan was a local farmer with a passion for racehorses. He had suffered grievously in a tractor accident and asked for my help. So, having delivered the children to school each morning, I would head to his place and ride out for an hour on sleek and muscular thoroughbreds. I would dismount feeling physically wrung out but all the more determined to make things happen back home. As a measure of my commitment, and because the local children kept knocking at my door, I even took on a few more horses to join Sparks and Roly.

Like the handsome specimens I rode out for John, Ginger was a cob from thoroughbred bloodstock. And yet he came with a catch that meant he wasn't priced out of my range. While his father was a respected stallion, Ginger's mother was a farm carthorse. I can't say for sure how he came into existence, but to my eyes my new addition to the Moyfield fold was a beauty, with a lovely, docile nature, and I took him on with a view to breeding horses of my own. In that time, I also acquired a Shetland mare called Mayfair. It wasn't just her health and character that attracted me, or the fact that her small size made her ideal for young riders; it was also the fact that she was in foal.

'All being well, that's two for the price of one,' I told Tony when I led her home.

Like Ginger, that horse quickly proved to be worth her weight in gold. Not only did Mayfair give birth to a lovely, even-tempered mare called Melody, she was a dream with even the most timid of children who took up the reins. With a swelling number of horses out in the field, it began to feel as if I had a school in the making.

'Joan,' declared Tony one day, when I talked once more of my plans. 'You already have a riding school! It started the moment those two little girls asked you for lessons, and it's been growing with the farm ever since!'

His outlook made me chuckle, but in a way he was right. With encouragement from my husband, I even took exams in riding tuition. By the time I qualified, and with certificates hanging from the wall, my dream had effectively come true.

For all our hard work over the years, however, there have been several occasions when trespassers threatened our idyll. Once, when we had only just moved into the bungalow, that threat arrived on four legs.

'He's paid another visit,' muttered Tony one morning, on returning from the poultry field. I was pregnant with Colin at the time, and we'd only recently established our flock. 'Damn it all, Joan!'

The thunder in his expression told me everything I needed to know about their fate.

'The fox?' I said. 'How many this time?'

Tony took a seat in the kitchen and removed his boots. I had been brewing a kettle on the stove when he walked in. The water was coming to the boil.

'It can't go on,' he said. 'Every laying hen it takes is costing us money we can't afford to lose.'

I took a moment to fill the pot. A cup of tea, I thought, would help to cool him down.

'Is it the same one?' I asked.

'Without a doubt,' said Tony. 'I've looked into its eyes once before.'

A few months earlier, we had been drawn by the sound of an anguished lowing from the calving field at Norval. There, the fox that Tony claimed to be responsible for the hen attack was attempting to drag a calf away by its foreleg. He wasn't successful, but only because Tony had grabbed the calf by its hind legs and entered into a macabre tug of war to save it. Ever since then, and following what was now the third attack on the hens, that fox had come to represent a threat to our livelihood.

'What do you have in mind?' I asked.

Tony took his tea from me in both hands.

'It has to be done, Joan,' he told me, and I knew just what he meant.

Like any farming household, with crops and livestock to protect, we kept shotguns. The twelve-bore required a steady aim and strong shoulder to support the kickback, while the .410 gauge was a little smaller but no less effective. As I considered the hens to be my responsibility, I insisted on accompanying Tony when he set out at sundown the next evening. He wasn't happy about it on two counts.

'You'd be better off with the .410,' he grumbled, as I walked out towards the wood alongside him with the twelve-bore broken open and crooked in my arm. 'Are you sure you can handle it?'

'I'm already carrying a child,' I reminded him on scanning the treeline. The shadows had deepened under the canopy, while the crimson band on the horizon defined the trunks and undergrowth. It was a long but thin copse, and we felt sure the fox's earth was in there. 'I dare say our son will protect me.'

Tony shot me a look; his gaze dropping momentarily to my belly.

'What makes you so sure it's a boy?'

'Because he's watching out for me,' I told him playfully. 'You'll see.'

★   ★   ★

We had heard the fox barking earlier. It's an unsettling sound, like a wailing widow, but having dealt with the aftermath of its last foray I was not to be deterred. As Tony had spotted a vixen trotting across this very field on several occasions, we worked on the basis that our quarry would be nearby.

'You go in from the top,' said Tony as we approached the trees. 'You'll be walking into the breeze so your scent won't give you away. I'll stand watch from the open. If it takes to the fields as you work your way through, I'll be ready.'

Tony was a proven shot from a distance, so it made sense to me. Bracing the gun stock and the muzzle, I made my way into the far end of the copse as quietly and steadily as I could. The bluebell season had only just come to an end. The wilting banks of stalks defined a deer track through the trees. I followed the path, looking up and around with every step. In woodland like this, when listening keenly, it's easy to think that a world of wildlife is aware of your presence. It took about ten minutes for me to reach the halfway mark. By then, I was ready to call out to Tony and suggest we look elsewhere.

When I drew breath, however, I did so in a gasp. For just when I was least expecting it, I came across our quarry. There it was, seemingly unaware of my presence, washing itself in a glade. Carefully, with my eyes locked on the fox, I braced the gunstock against my shoulder and took aim. With my scent covered, facing into the breeze, I was free to find my target in my sight and squeeze the trigger.

Only I couldn't bring myself to do it.

As soon as I levelled the gun, my hands began to tremble. The fox looked up, and stared right through me. I flexed my finger, willing myself to pull, but somehow the command refused to register. With a small cry of despair, having held my breath throughout, I lowered the gun.

The fox picked up on my presence right away. In a blink, it vanished into the undergrowth.

'Why did you spare it?' asked Tony, when I emerged into the open, but I just couldn't explain myself.

It was only later, when I gave birth to our boy, Colin, and the birthmark on his ankle became apparent, that I took it as some kind of sign. Even now, when I note that blemish, shaped as it is like a fox's head, I think back to that episode and feel somehow that I did the right thing. By sparing one life I had secured another.

Over the course of the following year, we spotted that sly old bugger a couple of times, but eventually he just vanished. Of course, four-legged thieves are a fact of life on a farm. It's all part of the tapestry when it comes to working the land. But it wouldn't be until many years later, when we received a visit from a thief of the two-legged variety, that I proved only a fox could have the measure of me.

'Excuse me, Missus,' said the man who had knocked at my door. 'One of your ponies is out on the lane. I can show you if you like?'

The man seemed pleasant enough. Wearing overalls, and with swept-back hair, greying at the temples, he looked like a typical farm-hand. The only thing that marked him out, I noted as I hurried down the drive with him, was the manner of his walk. He had a strange kind of swagger, but more immediately I shared his concern that a loose horse on the road could cause an accident.

'Where did you see it?' I asked.

'Up here, Missus.' He gestured beyond the meadowland towards the village. I could see no horse, however. 'Maybe he's trotted to the shops!'

I smiled at his comment, but the further we walked the more uncertain I became.

'Are you sure?' I asked.

'Quite sure, Missus. This way!'

As he said this, I was struck by a very bad feeling. I glanced back over my shoulder. In the distance, little more than specks, I saw two figures prowling around the bungalow as if looking for a way in.

'What's going on?' I asked, and stopped dead in my tracks. 'Who are you? There's no horse out here!'

The man faced around, but continued walking backwards. He looked stricken all of a sudden. As I raised my voice to repeat myself, he turned and ran.

By the time I raced back to the drive, the pair had already fled the bungalow and were sprinting across the field. We had been robbed of money from the riding club and jewellery that I couldn't afford to lose. I blamed myself entirely.

'I've been a fool!' I told Tony, but he would hear none of it.

Despite his assurance that it could've happened to anyone, I felt entirely responsible. We recovered a necklace that had been dropped by the thieves as they fled, but the episode would've haunted me were it not for a call from the local police station some days later. Not only had they traced the van, and recovered the equipment, but they had a suspect in custody and asked if I could identify him.

'Do you recognise anyone in this line up, Ma'am?' asked the officer when I went in. 'Any faces ring a bell?'

I looked along the line. None of them stood out. They all looked like regular farm-hands, and the police had done a thorough job of selecting men with swept-back, greying hair. Then I had an idea.

'Could you ask them to walk for me?' I requested, and then nodded with absolute certainty when one chap did so with a swagger.

21

The Bomford Boys

Coming of age.

For livestock farmers like us, market day was once a regular feature in the calendar that promised a return for all our hard work. To an outsider, it could seem like a mystifying place populated by noisy, jostling bovines and men in smocks who appeared to jabber in tongues. Having attended markets since I was little, however, it seemed totally natural to me.

Father used to take me to nearby venues like Gloucester and Worcester. Here, the old boys would gather around a sawdust ring where cattle, as well as sheep, pigs and poultry, were put up for sale or auction. There was money to be made here, but you couldn't just take that for granted.

After I married Tony, and began working with the Moyfield herd, we were always mindful to attend a market that could give us the best price. Tony and his father's pedigree dairy cows had a reputation for providing good milk yields. Here at Norval the herd was fed a diet of hay and a processed feed in pellet form called cake. When cows were fed silage, a fermented fodder often favoured by farmers with plenty of available grass crops, the milk yield would always go up. So it made good business sense for us to sell at markets in the north of England, where counties such as Cheshire are favoured by a slightly warmer and wetter climate due to the gulf stream.

The challenge, of course, lay in transporting our livestock to places as far afield as Uttoxeter and Crewe. In our early day at the bungalow, when our savings for the riding school were regularly diminished in order to support our infant farm, we bought a Bedford truck. It was an expensive vehicle, but would come to earn its keep for years as a trusted livestock transporter. With a journey that could take up to five hours, Tony and I would pull down the cattle ramp, load up the lorry and travel to the market the day before. We could transport half a dozen cows in the Bedford, but with such a long journey their welfare was paramount. It meant driving smoothly at a steady speed, and without stopping if we could possibly help it. When the children were very little we'd often have to take them with us. Naturally, someone would be pleading for a loo break before we'd even cleared the Vale, so it often proved to be a merry old challenge.

At the end of each long day on the road, we'd frequently find ourselves in traffic with other livestock vehicles as we approached the market. They were big, popular venues, and once inside we couldn't afford to hang around and chat. The cattle would have to be unloaded immediately, and then fed, watered and washed down before being settled into pens. Back home, our cows would be milked first thing in the morning and at the end of the day. On the eve of a farmers' market, we would skip the second milking so their bags would fill overnight. In terms of presentation, it would show a potential buyer just what our cattle could deliver. Once every cow was settled, and the Bedford truck swept out, we would head off to our lodgings for a hot bath and a well-earned sleep ahead of the big day.

Of course, in the morning the cattle would need washing down all over again. We'd even give them a good shampoo, and make sure the head collar that we'd use to lead them out was polished up and gleaming. The old farmers' markets would often incorporate a judging show, with prizes on offer across all classes of livestock. As a rosette or two could make a big difference in sale price, we always made every effort to present our cattle in the best shape possible. The same went for Tony and me. As sellers, we had to meet the same standards of presentation, which meant scrubbed boots and starched white smocks. We put these on at the last minute, of course, for just being around livestock is enough to earn a few specks of muck on your clothing. Then, ahead of our turn in the ring, we would give our cows a friendly pat and prepare to parade them out.

As soon as that moment arrived, one of us would enter the ring with our head held high, leading livestock we had raised to the very best of our abilities. Often standing upon a platform or gallery, the auctioneer would host proceedings with the skill, timing and control of an orchestral conductor. All we could do was hold our breath until the reserve price was met, and then have faith in the quality of our cattle to see the bidding figure rise.

People often ask me if I can understand the auctioneer at farmers' markets. Listening to them acknowledging each bid so quickly, it can certainly sound like nonsense. Then again, when your livelihood depends on it you develop a strong sense of focus and a very keen ear.

After most visits, we would drive home with an empty truck. On other occasions, whether or not it was planned, our return to the Vale would be marked by a new addition. One of us would set eyes on a calf or a heifer and just know that it was destined to graze on our fields. As well as seeing our cattle numbers grow, Tony and I brought a fourth and final child into the world. Kim was born in May 1965. Joining her older sister and two brothers, she very quickly proved to be a daddy's girl and a tomboy in spirit. While Marie showed a natural talent for riding ponies, Kim would often be found with Tony whilst he was milking. As for my boys, two little rascals who always did us proud, they discovered that growing up on a farm meant taking on roles and responsibilities that occasionally far outshone their years.

'But Dad,' said Colin, when Tony had laid out his plan for the boys one weekend. 'I'm only twelve.'

'You're old enough to drive a tractor in the fields,' his father reminded him. 'In my book, that makes you more than capable of selling cattle at market on your own.'

'In Crewe?' Colin didn't sound so sure. 'That's a long way to go on my own.'

'You won't be alone.' Tony summoned Colin's younger brother from his spot on the floor in front of the TV. 'Joe will be going with you.'

Usually, when Tony travelled north, he relied on a stockman back at Norval to help his father with the milking duties. As Ken was off sick, and with my blessing, he turned to his oldest son for support.

'But what if something goes wrong?' asked Colin, which made Tony smile and ruffle his hair.

'Nothing will go wrong,' he assured him. 'You'll head up there as a Bomford boy, and return as a young man.'

I trusted Tony to make sure that Joe and Colin would manage. We knew plenty of farmers who attended the market at Crewe, as well as friendly staff. I also wrote a letter for the hotel where I had reserved a double room for them, which included our contact details should anyone need to reach us. I was worried, of course. As a mother, it's only natural. But I was also so busy back at Moyfield that all I could do was place the same faith in my sons as their father showed them.

Tony sent up four cows to sell that weekend. Colin and his brother helped him to load them onto the Bedford, before I waved them off from the drive.

'Don't get into mischief,' I called out over the engine as the lorry trundled by.

'What was that?' Joe cupped his ear, grinning broadly, and then faced the front as their father pulled out into the lane.

On arriving at Crewe, with the sun setting over the town's civic buildings, Tony eased the truck through the market gates and prepared to hand over to his sons.

'Once we've unloaded you're on your own,' he told them.

For once, Joe didn't look so jolly.

'When will you be back?' he asked.

'The same time tomorrow,' he promised. 'All you need to do is let me know if I should bring the truck or the car.'

Colin knew full well that he was expected to sell all four cattle. Just then, however, I expect he was more concerned by the fact that he was about to be left in sole charge of his brother in a town that seemed like hundreds of miles from home.

'Good luck,' said Tony, from the driver's seat, and left them both with a wink before steering the truck out into the dusk.

It took both boys a good three hours to wash down the cattle and settle them in for the night. Tony had left the pair with a bucket and body brushes, and freshly laundered smocks folded into their suitcases. Just then, however, as a first experience of managing such responsibilities alone, Colin struggled to work out where to leave the cleaning equipment overnight.

'It might get pinched,' he said fretfully, clutching the bucket as if it were the crown jewels.

'We could take it with us,' Joe suggested.

Colin dismissed the suggestion out of hand.

'We can't check into a hotel with a bucket,' he said. 'Mum would go mad.'

Joe looked around. While most of the farmers were finishing bedding down their livestock, some had already gone. He turned his attention to a stall across the aisle that contained a sleeping pig. A bale of straw had been left against the wall behind it. Through the eyes of my eight-year-old son, that pig would serve as a fitting watchman for our cleaning equipment. So, having stashed it all behind the bale, and leaving the pig in charge, my sons set off to find their own beds for the night.

A revolving door stood between Colin, Joe and the hotel lobby. Standing on the pavement under the stars, with their little suitcases at their sides, the boys watched guests coming and going for a moment.

'Joe,' said Colin after a moment. 'Don't even think about it.'

Even at twelve, Colin knew his little brother only too well. When faced with the opportunity to clown about, they were both as bad as each other, but generally Joe would be first.

'Just once around,' he insisted, before stepping up to the door as it turned and slipping into the first available segment.

Of course, with his suitcase in hand it was inevitable that Joe would get the thing wedged. Colin watched, grim-faced, as his little brother attempted in vain to free the case. Finally, he stepped up to snatch it away before leaving Joe to go full circle with a clip about the head. Once inside, with the bags intact, the pair were momentarily overcome by the sheer size of the lobby. It was big, but not too grand, and above all it was safe for two guests of their tender age. When visiting as a family, we had often stayed there on market trips, and always been made to feel very welcome.

'This is from my parents,' said Colin, and presented the letter to the receptionist. As he waited for her to read it, a crash drew his attention to the fact that Joe had just taken a step back to admire the ceiling rose and promptly tripped over his case. He turned to the receptionist once again and smiled sweetly. 'Is it too late to ask for single rooms?'

The next morning, both boys were deeply relieved to find the pig had done a fine job of guarding their bucket and brushes. With only a short time before the auction was due to begin, they came into their own that morning. Having cleaned the cattle, and ensured the head collar was polished and fitted, it was Colin who elected to unpack his white smock and lead the cows into the ring. As Joe looked on, craning to see from behind the bidding farmers, his older brother sold three cows one after the other.

The fourth, however, failed to meet the reserve price.

The cow was in just as fine shape as the others, but with several bidders out of the frame there just wasn't sufficient demand left. Reluctantly, Colin led the unwanted lot from the ring. As he did so, he caught the eye of the auctioneer.

'Drop the reserve and I can sell it straight away,' the man suggested, having clearly taken pity on this young lad and his brother.

Colin looked to Joe, who shook his head. Both of them knew that their father was canny about the value of his cattle. They would do better to bring it home than confess they had undersold it.

'If we wait until the end,' Colin suggested instead, 'can you put her in again at the same reserve price?'

Within the hour, our eldest son was on the phone to his father, asking him to collect them in the car.

With an afternoon to kill, and feeling very pleased with themselves, our boys decided to treat themselves to a trip to the pictures. There, with open mouths, they watched Michael Caine under siege and outnumbered in *Zulu*. Such was their enchantment with the film that neither of them cared that their father was an hour later than planned. When he finally pulled up in the Ford Consul that we owned at the time, and explained that he'd been pulled over twice as the car matched a vehicle wanted in connection with a bank robbery, the boys must've wondered whether their grand adventure would ever end.

22

Building a Dream

The 'Ponderosa'.

When Tony put up the signage at the end of the driveway, I knew that we had made it.

'There,' he said, standing back with me to admire the hand-painted white board that still stands proud today. 'Moyfield Riding School & Club.'

'Open all year,' I added, reading out the line we had included underneath.

'Come rain or shine.' Tony grinned and took my arm to escort me back to the venture we had built from scratch. With hard work, time and patience, we had taken a field of rough grassland on the outlying land of Norval farm and transformed it. This wasn't just a home any longer. We offered a way of life for riders with a passion who couldn't afford to own horses of their own. As a couple, Tony and I were older and wiser for the experience, but still very much in love and passionate about our undertaking. What with all his responsibilities, Tony's crop of hair had begun to lose its dark colouring, and yet life for us continued to blossom and shine. Not only did I take on more ponies to cope with demand, I even opened the bungalow doors to all the young riders and treated them as my own. Those early years at Moyfield were enchanting, while Tony had his work cut out to accommodate both rider and horse. By then, whenever he wasn't managing the dairy herd at Norval, looking after our burgeoning bloodstock or swinging children from his shoulders, he was hard at work fencing and building on our land.

'We can't keep adding stables at the back,' said Tony, when I asked him to extend our block of ten by another three. 'We've almost reached the hedgerow!'

'Then what about a barn?' I asked, and drew his attention to the field adjacent to our little lawn. Since we had taken on Ginger, that cob had been busy sowing his wild oats. We had put him with a mare called Brandy, who got in foal straight away, while a gate left open by accident some months earlier meant he'd serviced several more of my horses. Around that time, Tony had built a garage at the top of the drive. Having acquired the Bedford lorry, at great expense, to transport our cattle, he'd constructed a spacious timber frame and clad it to keep our investment in the dry. Then Ginger had increased my head count of horses, and within weeks the truck had been displaced from the garage in favour of pony pens.

Tony himself had suggested the original stable block. He just hadn't counted on the steady rise in customers, and my commitment to providing horses that weren't exhausted from being ridden every hour of the day. Building a barn, rather than extending the block still further, seemed a more sensible option to him as much as me. In my experience, horses kept together in such an environment were more relaxed and content, and their welfare has always been my priority.

The challenge, as it became apparent to us both once we had drawn up a plan, lay in the sheer size of the structure we had in mind. In order to shelter the horses, and cater for the steady increase in our stock, we would need a very big building indeed. Tony knew that he could call upon a local pair of hands to help him with the breezeblock walls, but with such a large square footage the roof required columns and joists at a considerable height.

'As I see it we have three options,' he said, 'Number one, Colin is old enough to climb onto my shoulders and heave them into place.'

'You're joking,' I said, and rolled my eyes when Tony confirmed that he was.

'Second, we could hire scaffolding to get the job done, but we could have it here on site for quite some time and that's a luxury we can't afford.'

'A luxury?' Tony and I were standing in the space behind the garage that we had earmarked for the barn. 'It sounds like scaffolding is the only way to get the roof on.'

Tony responded as if I had overseen an obvious solution.

'We're farmers,' he said to remind me. 'And we farmers are a resourceful bunch.'

I was so busy with lessons that I didn't pay his plans any further thought. As the walls went up, I admired the work and looked forward to sheltering all my horses under one roof. In those rare moments when we had time together, Tony and I would visit the pictures in town. We were especially fond of Westerns. John Wayne was my hero, not to mention the name of a bull Tony would one day keep in a cattle field of ours, but above all I admired the way those cowboys cared for their horses. I recognised the bond they forged, and undertook to do the same thing. Keeping them together at night struck me as the most natural thing to do. But first Tony had to finish it.

'What on earth are you boys doing?' I asked one afternoon, on finding Colin and little Joe helping his dad heave straw bales onto the site. The walls had gone up beautifully, but with the rain we'd had the ground was a mud-bath.

Tony grinned at me as he passed by, shouldering a bale.

'Scaffolding,' he said, and set his straw load beside another one. 'The natural way.'

Curious, I watched for a while as they filled the floor with bales. By the time I had gone off to run a lesson, and returned with cups of tea, the floor had grown to become six bales high.

'Oh, no,' I said in horror. 'That can't be safe, can it?'

'It's safe enough. So long as I don't move around too much.'

'For a man who insists I keep my insurance up to date on the riding school,' I said, 'you're taking quite a risk.'

'We need to take care of our customers,' he said with a wink. 'You and I just take our chances. It's got us this far, after all.'

'Tony,' I called out, as the bales he was using as steps to the top of his straw platform shifted under his weight. 'Will you get down from there?'

From the summit, ready to haul up another bale from the boys, my husband asked me to have a little faith.

'I'm here to build a roof,' he assured me, and pointed upwards. 'And a roof you shall get.'

'That's fine,' I said, 'but I'd also like a husband at the end of it.'

With bales laid around his makeshift platform, just in case he should fall off, Tony promised that Joe would stay at ground level – in charge of the nails – while insisting that Colin was old enough to assist him with the task at hand. It was painstaking work, and not because it involved expanding the platform as they fixed timber pillars and tin sheets in place. Frankly, however, I was too busy and anxious to watch. Over the next few days, I heard a great deal of heaving and hammering, not to mention the cursing whenever Tony flattened his thumb, and yet my husband and sons persevered. When they finally invited me to venture out behind the garage, I had nothing but admiration for their achievement.

'It's quite safe,' declared Tony, who had cut some bale strings and used some straw to cover the floor. He stood in the heart of the new barn, his voice echoing under the corrugated roof. Colin and Joe were already packing up the tools, clearly confident in the quality of their father's work, so I joined Tony in the middle and thanked him with a kiss.

That barn was the beginning of many more buildings at Moyfield Riding School and Club. Tony's newfound confidence led to the creation of a shed for the tractor and the hay, a row of calf pens and another stable block opposite the bungalow, as well as an indoor riding arena using the very same bale-balancing technique as before, which caused my heart to quicken yet again. In effect, the school became a little kingdom of our own, spread across several acres, and increasingly teeming with life and laughter.

My husband's finest creation, perhaps, stands proud in the garden behind the bungalow. The miniature ranch house, nestled between plants and bushes, was acquired from a caravan park by Tony, and repurposed to serve as a tack room. It's no more than a generous beach hut in size, with one side marked for the boys' equipment, and the other for the girls', but over the years it has come to mark the beating heart of our little riding venture. For this is where the young students gathered to get ready for their lessons, and chatter about their lives. With two rooms at the back, which would come to be fitted with bunks, there was always something going on in there, and I adored it. Best of all was the name that it acquired. Everyone called that tack room the Ponderosa, after the ranch in the family's favourite TV Western, *Bonanza*.

Every week, when the show aired, my children and some of the stable staff would gather in front of our big old TV to watch the exploits of the Cartwright family, and imagine they were living similar lives. In many ways, Moyfield offered the same kind of opportunities with our horses and wild open spaces. On one occasion, as none of us will ever forget, the show even came a little too close to our existence for comfort.

'It's on!' Marie shouted to her siblings as the signature music began. I was cooking tea at the time, and knew that it would keep them occupied for the next thirty minutes. 'Joe? Kim? Colin? *Bonanza* is starting!'

I'd sat with them enough times to know that the opening credits began with a map of the Cartwright's vast landholding. As the music played out, a flame would slowly eat through the map, peeling away on both sides like theatre curtains to reveal the family on horseback. Just then, the other three rushed in from the garden with no time to kick off their shoes.

'Mum!'

I ignored Marie's appeal as I cooked, with the music still ringing out from the front room. Whatever she wanted, I thought, she needed to learn to come and address me politely rather than just yelling. Then Marie called out again, more urgently this time, and that's when I smelled burning.

'Mum!' she cried a third time. 'The TV is on fire!'

That poor girl must've been so confused. There she sat as her siblings and a string of stable girls joined her, braced for the map to burn away before the opening scene began, when our television chose that same moment to short and start an electrical blaze.

Fortunately, in the scramble that followed, I managed to make sure that everyone escaped unscathed into the garden. That evening, instead of watching an episode of their treasured show, those young-sters in my care witnessed the fire brigade in action. The smoke caused most damage, as it turned out, but I was just thankful that everyone was safe. It was some time before we could afford to replace the TV. By then, however, the children were pursuing their own adventures in and around the riding school. With more cus-tomers, more horses, and a small army of stable girls to support me, I found myself running an operation that went beyond my wildest imagination. Nothing, I believed, could take the wind out of our sails. Except, perhaps, the wind itself.

I don't recall the precise year that the gale swept in, but it howled over the Vale all night long and peeled off the roof of the riding school. We ventured out in the morning to find buckled sheets of corrugated tin lying around like giant strips of fried bacon. Friends and customers helped to clear the debris, but Tony was not to be defeated by the elements. This time, however, and much to my relief, he took the opportunity to hire professional workers to help him out. Most reassuringly of all, they supplied their own scaffolding.

23

The Boom Years

My children − Colin, Marie and Joe with baby Kim.

With one hundred acres to farm on his own, my brother stepped out of Dad's shadow and into a strengthening sun.

John Collins had learned everything from Father, and though he missed him as much as everyone else, he embraced his calling with the very same tenacity and conviction that our dad had shown. Advances in agricultural machinery might have eclipsed steam power when it came to working the land, but Brother was a man with a keen appreciation of traditional farming methods. The engines he took over from Father weren't gleaming like the latest tractors of the time, but they served to do a job and do it well, and that informed his approach to life.

John still ploughed and scuffled the fields at Quarry Pits with a crew and the two Fowlers, but he also developed an innovative land-drainage business that kept both his men and machines busy. It was a service that proved popular with groundsmen who had no wish to spoil their playing fields and football pitches. Instead, they would watch with a sense of wonder and admiration as John and his team threaded pipes under the ground from one side to the other. Those Fowlers were dirty and noisy beasts, but by God under pressure they could haul or drag a bore through heavy clay like a knife through butter.

With his cattle and crops, as well as a newfound role for his ageing engines, Brother proved to be yet another generation of the Collins family who recognised the reward that came from working the soil. He proved to be knowledgeable and wise, and was as passionate about the welfare of his livestock as he was about his steam tackle. With decades of service at Quarry Pits, local farmers often called upon his advice. A fair-minded man, always with a practical eye, John once went into a joint deal with a neighbouring farmer for a delivery of solid oak planks from the local timber yard. Both had outbuildings in mind of some sort, but John calculated with impressive accuracy that they would be left with a small surplus. With no return policy, and rather than leave them to rot, he offered to store them for later use.

'There are enough planks here to build two coffins,' he said. 'Whatever happens to us in life, we'll be needing them one day.'

As for Mother, in her widowhood she found comfort in books.

Kitty Collins had always enjoyed reading when we were younger, but the demands of running a busy household left her little time to herself. With Father gone, and her children grown up, she sought the company of stories. Quarry Pits might have become quieter, but her imagination remained as full of life as the place where we grew up.

My sister, Marian, remained her constant companion. She had left school with exemplary qualifications, and a clear conviction that her calling would go no further than the farmhouse. As a young woman, she had come to recognise that her life belonged within those red brick walls, and though people were surprised they came to respect her commitment. There, with no yearning to seek new pastures, she happily devoted herself to cooking, cleaning, sewing and gardening. In many ways she came into her own at Quarry Pits after Dad passed away. For that's when Mother retreated from the domestic frontline she had occupied throughout the years.

While the three members of my family back at the farmhouse moved on in different ways, they would unite with smiles and happiness when visiting us at Moyfield. John and Marian adored their nephews and nieces, and the children felt the same way about their uncle and aunt. As for Kitty Collins, it was a joy to watch her spend time with Marie, Colin, Joe and Kim, and the same went for Irene.

My mother-in-law had set out to make my married life as difficult as possible. She didn't like me to begin with, and felt that her son could've done better. I was forever mindful that only a girl like Margaret, the vicar's girl, would've met Irene's standards by providing her son with a step up in the world. Instead, he had chosen me, the daughter of another farmer, and Irene struggled to deal with the fact that we made each other happy.

In response, all I could do was be true to the family I raised with Tony, and hope she would come round. The death of my father certainly proved to be a turning point in our relationship. Irene was genuinely remorseful about denying me that final chance to say goodbye to him. For all her small acts of cruelty, she did at least come to consider this a step too far, and sought to change her ways from that moment on. We were never the very best of friends, but we tolerated one another politely and always with respect. As a grandmother, however, she was adored, and I admired the commitment she and Trevor made to the children. While I had seen how she could cool the emotional temperature in a room, around them she brought only warmth, generosity, encouragement and love.

But it wasn't just my four kids that made Moyfield such a joyful place to be. As a riding school, each year saw more and more youngsters enrol for lessons. They came from far and wide, not just the local villages but cities like Birmingham, Coventry and London, too. Older pupils also made enquiries, and they were equally welcome. Having qualified to teach at every level, I encouraged individuals of all ages and ability into the saddle. In my experience, riding can have a transformative effect on people. I took one little lad under my wing who had lived with muscular problems since birth. His parents, close friends of ours, had taken him to see consultants as far afield as Sheffield. It was during a conversation with his father that I learned one doctor had recommended climbing up and down a ladder on a daily basis, or horse riding.

'Then he should ride,' I said.

'Joan,' he replied. 'We just couldn't afford it.'

I considered him with a smile.

'I never mentioned money,' I told him.

To witness that boy come alive in the saddle during his time at the school is something I shall never forget. Movement was a challenge for him when he first arrived, but he left with a new lease of life. From the elderly and disabled, to the lost, the wayward and distressed, people discovered a purpose and direction in riding my horses that perhaps they couldn't find in other aspects of their lives.

As well as the school, our riding club went from strength to strength.

Weekends were often devoted to gymkhanas. There was always something going on, and if I didn't know about an event then one of the children would soon draw it to my attention. On Saturday or Sunday mornings at dawn, I'd load up the lorry with ponies, seat a group of excited and chattering children in the front, and off we'd go for a day of trotting, cantering, jumping, judging and rosettes. My daughter, Kim, loved her time at these events. Once, she found herself representing the North Cotswolds Pony Club in the Prince Philip Cup Games. I was so proud of her.

Above all, everyone adored the school holidays. That's when we took on young riders for a week or more, and they would come to live with us as family. Of course, we didn't have enough space in the bungalow, which prompted Tony to take his toolkit inside the Ponderosa and expand its function from a simple tack room. With enough space to squeeze in beds for eight girls, this is where friendships were forged that endure to this day. He also attached another shed to the back, known as the bunk house, and that housed up to six boys at a time. We brought in several wagons and caravans as well, and arranged them around the grounds at the back in a corral formation. With a place for everyone to lay their heads at night, my young holiday club riders gained their first taste of independence, and revelled in the experience.

Of course, with so many guests sleeping in the garden, we needed toilet facilities. Any club member who has ever spent time at Moyfield will be sure to smile when they remember our outside WC: the poetically named, Poo Send. This was simply a wooden hut with a galvanised steel bucket inside, fitted with a seat. Although nobody complained about the facility, there was little love lost for the loo paper Tony always stocked. Everyone compared it to tracing paper. Later, he would cave in and plumb in a flushing toilet at the back of the Ponderosa, while his decision to clip a roll of soft loo roll to the wall was no doubt met by sighs of relief from the occupants.

Then there were my young grooms. Through the holidays in the 1970s and into the 80s, I often had up to eight young women at a time to assist and support me. In return for helping out at the riding school, I provided full board and lodging, just as I did for our holiday club members, which meant finding them somewhere to sleep.

'The bungalow,' suggested Tony, when the problem first arose.

'But every room is fit to burst,' I pointed out.

'Not up there,' he said, and pointed to the ceiling.

And so, following a loft conversion by my hardworking husband, whose hair was turning whiter by the season, the grooms would climb a ladder to sleep in the roof at night, and also take their turn to eat at the dining-room table.

With so many mouths to feed, at breakfast, lunch and supper, we had to organise a shift system. We squeezed twelve chairs around the table, and I made sure that nobody went hungry by serving over three sittings. It was important to me that everyone ate well. If they wanted to make the most of their time at the riding school, they needed a full belly with decent food. So I cooked a lot of rabbit stews. Unlike the evacuees, who frankly had too much time on their hands, the youngsters at my table would clear their plates without fail, and often request second helpings.

Those holiday clubs would have so many high points for the children, often unplanned or unexpected. There was the time one late afternoon, I remember, when a hot-air balloon came down in one of the fields. It caused the horses to scatter, of course, while drawing youngsters from every quarter of the school. To make up for the trouble caused, not that it was anything but entertaining, I even received a free flight. Another year, a glider landed in a field where we were growing wheat. Tony was less than delighted by that unexpected landing, but it taught us all that anything could happen at Moyfield Riding School and Club, and such incidents gave the children a magical memory to take home with them.

Many of our members kept in touch long after they left, and would continue to write to us as adults. From time to time, we'd receive a lovely letter from some far-flung region of the world with a faded Polaroid enclosed of a moment at Moyfield that we had shared together. Whatever path in life those kids had gone on to take, it was so nice to learn that they considered their time with us as the platform that allowed them to spread their wings.

Apart from the odd occasion when someone took a tumble from the saddle, the only time we saw anybody cry was when the holidays came to an end. With such basic amenities, and all their efforts devoted to riding, eating or sleeping, it's fair to say that those spirited urchins were so dirty at the end that they proved largely unrecognisable to the parents who came to collect them. Nobody ever asked to go home early. If anything, they were desperate to stay longer, and we would have to placate them by reminding them that the club would always be here in the holidays for as long as they kept on coming. Nothing would stop their lower lips from wobbling, however, when it came to saying goodbye to the ponies they had ridden throughout their stay. That's when things became emotional, not just for the children but for the mums and dads who could see how much it meant to them. As soon as they arrived, it was obvious that their little one had been through an intense farewell by the tear-tracks down their grubby, sun-freckled cheeks.

Those were such special days, I think to myself whenever I look through my photograph albums. They bring back such happy memories spanning almost twenty years. At one point, with the school running full tilt, I kept upwards of one hundred horses, most of which I bred myself. It was only in the late 1990s, when technology evolved once more and brought the Internet to our homes, that demand for the holiday clubs began to dwindle. I suppose the web helped families become aware of other activities and pastimes, while the draw of the great outdoors has perhaps lost its attraction to a generation with entertainment at their fingertips. The club caravans and wagons are still here, and sometimes I swear that I hear laughter from the Ponderosa. No doubt it's just the breeze, or my imagination playing tricks, but it always makes me smile when I reflect upon a time our family call the boom years. I still teach at the school, of course. There's always someone new who wants to learn how to ride. Whether they're young, old, rich or poor, and from whatever walk of life, I intend to provide a welcome for them here for the rest of my days.

24
Battles

Riding into battle.

To live off the land, in any shape or form, you have to adapt to the times.

John had found a way to keep the fireboxes burning inside the traction engines, and Quarry Pits continued to provide for my mother and Marian. In the same way, when the riding school became central to my life, and took up all my time, I decided to finish with our market garden. It had been good to us in the early days, and helped to finance the bungalow and the very early phase of the school. But by the time I had so many horses that space was at a premium, I knew that the land would serve us better as pasture.

It was a shame to stop planting out vegetable crops and watching them grow, but I had to follow my farming instinct for survival. While our wonderful holiday clubs were still going strong, I could sense that they wouldn't last forever. We were still full to capacity, but the waiting list was beginning to shorten each season. With

Tony's commitments increasing over at the dairy farm, as my father-in-law grew older, I knew it was down to me to open up new avenues.

What I couldn't have known back then was that our saving grace would see my horses effectively travel back in time by three hundred years.

As well as taking my club members to compete in gymkhanas, I would occasionally invite older and more experienced riders on bigger challenges. Sometimes this would involve a drive across the country for a trekking adventure that could last up to several days. One event in particular will always bring me fond memories. The Golden Horseshoe has been running annually for over fifty years now, and invites endurance competitors to trek across one hundred miles of Exmoor wilderness. Both horse and rider have to be in extremely good shape, and the challenge demands both stamina and a brisk, steady pace. I took it very seriously, and instilled a clear understanding among my team of the test that they would face. The weather could be unpredictable, the terrain both rugged and sometimes steep, and exhaustion would be sure to accompany them in the saddle. They would be expected to negotiate tumbling streams, thread their way through wooded coombes and cross wide open heath carpeted with heather.

'In short,' I promised them all, 'it'll be an experience that you'll treasure for the rest of your lives.'

By the time we arrived for the event, the seven riders under my care were well prepared, as were their horses. We had undertaken several treks in order to qualify, and exercised the horses for several hours a day throughout the preceding month. Everyone was in good shape both physically and mentally, and I was well aware of my responsibilities. These mature students had put their trust in their steed and me as we set off on a trail like no other. As a result, I made sure that we rode in a tight group and maintained a certain distance from those behind us. In my experience, horses could be unsettled and even startled if they found themselves overtaken, and I didn't want to risk any of my group being thrown from the saddle.

As I had promised, over the course of two days, every single one of those hundred miles proved memorable. We had a fabulous time, despite aching limbs, and finished with smiles on our faces. The Golden Horseshoe has always been quite an event. Plenty of people came out to watch, and at one point I was asked for an interview by a local BBC radio station. They wanted to know all about our preparation, and how I had selected the seven horses from the stock available at my school. I remember speaking with great pride about my riding companions, with no sense that the broadcast was set to change the course of my life.

A few days after we returned to the Vale, I received a telephone call. The man introduced himself as a representative of a historical association dedicated to the re-enactment of costumed battles.

'We're looking for someone who can provide a number of well-trained horses,' he told me. 'You sound like just the lady we've been looking for!'

The event he had in mind, which he described for me in detail, was like nothing I had heard of before. The association boasted hundreds of members ready to dress up in period dress from the English Civil War, and recreate a famous conflict for the entertainment of the public. It was all undertaken while making the safety and welfare of both horse and rider a priority, which is why he had called me. In the past, he explained, they had approached small stables which had only been able to offer a couple of horses each.

'And when put together those horses didn't get along,' I said with some certainty, which stopped the man in his tracks.

'How did you know?' he asked with a sigh, as if the memory of some recent experience still pained him.

I told the man I lived for horses, and that I'd be delighted to take up his offer. Not only did it sound like a new and interesting experience; the work on offer also came with a fee, and the upkeep of my school was uppermost in mind.

When I told Tony about the proposition, he raised an issue that I had already considered.

'The noise,' he said, having heard of such events. 'There'll be cannons, muskets and all sorts. Those soldiers might be firing blanks, but what if it startles the horses?'

'It won't,' I said, and reminded him of the preparations we had once undertaken when a local theatre company had called upon our services. They were staging a production of the musical, *Oklahoma*, and required a real horse for the stage. We had selected our most compliant mare, and then spent weeks in advance playing loud music and banging an oil drum in her presence. It didn't take long for her to settle, until we reached a point where there was no sound that could disturb her. On stage, she proved to be a star.

'If you're going to get every horse ready in time,' said Tony, 'then you had better add noise-making to your stable girls' list of duties.'

Well, it made lessons interesting for a few weeks. My students would climb into the saddle and ask why my girls were walking around the school thumping tins with sticks. Anything that made a racket, and would potentially startle a horse, we tried out until they learned not to be alarmed. Eventually, with hard work and persistence, I had a school of horses that could've continued to graze contentedly had a fleet of bombers swept over the Vale.

My next challenge lay in delivering the horses to the event. As the re-enactment association had hired as many as I could provide, and with the battle due to take place in the grounds of Sudeley Castle in Gloucestershire, I spent much of the final week shuttling up and down the road in the lorry. It was hard work, not just in covering so many journeys behind the wheel but in stabling my horses in temporary accommodation and taking good care of them.

On the morning of the event, with Kim and Marie at my side

along with several stable girls, I was up before dawn with the horses. They needed feeding, mucking out, saddling up and effectively preparing for battle. The grounds were huge, fenced off around the perimeter with entry points for the crowds who had come to watch the spectacle. Colin had just turned twenty at the time. Along with Joe, having heard me talk about the planned spectacle, he had driven down to watch. While the girls and I marshalled the horses away from public view, they joined the crowds overlooking an area that had been mocked up to look like a seventeenth-century village. There, amateur actors and actresses dressed as serfs, wenches and farm-hands pretended to go about their daily lives.

'I don't know about you,' Colin said at one point, having watched a succession of carts trundle by, 'but I'm quite bored.'

Joe was never one to complain, but even he shared the same sentiments as his brother. There was no doubt that people had gone to a great deal of effort to recreate this scene of pastoral life, but nothing much was actually happening.

'I'm glad I didn't live in these times,' muttered Joe, kicking idly at the grass at his feet. 'Give me the Wild West any day.'

Colin took in their surroundings. Some way behind him stood the castle. It overlooked well-kept gardens that swept out to fields and the makeshift village, before the land rose towards a ridge beyond. Had my boys known what was gathering behind that ridge, they might've changed their tune.

'Are you all quite ready?' I asked the sixty-strong cavalry brigade that had gathered on horseback before me. Dressed in full regalia, they really were a sight to behold, but I had a job to do here and the time to admire the spectacle could wait. 'As seasoned riders, you'll know that a horse responds best to calm authority.'

Arranged in a loose crescent, the volunteers nodded while focusing on keeping their charges steady. With legions of pikemen milling around, preparing to get into formation, the horses were picking up on the mounting excitement. I had been assured that every rider present had plenty of experience in the saddle. I just wasn't sure how much, but as the call went out for the brigade to get into position just behind the crest of the rise, all I could do was clear out of the way. From there on out my role was to walk behind them and take care of any horse should it lose a rider and bolt. It took a couple of minutes for the volunteers to assemble into line. I felt my nerves rising, simply because my horses looked primed as if preparing for a race.

'Good luck,' I called out, as a herald with a trumpet signalled for the charge to begin.

On the other side of the crest, behind the village where the crowds had gathered, Colin and Joe heard the trumpet loud and clear. Along with everyone else, including the villagers, they turned their attention to the crest of the rise. At the same time, a sound like rolling thunder began to build from beyond. The sight of the first few pikemen served to focus the spectators, who promptly gasped at the sheer size of the force that then spread across the summit. When the battle cry went up, my two sons glanced at one another.

'Do you remember that film we saw up at Crewe one year?' asked Colin. 'When Dad dumped us with four cows to sell at market.'

'*Zulu?*' said Joe without taking his eyes off the rise.

'That's the one …'

As the pikemen began to charge down the rise, the first wave of riders galloped over the crest behind them. They looked like surging ants from where the boys were standing, only for several to suddenly fly from their saddles.

'Have they been shot?' asked Joe in awe, as the crackle of muskets accompanied the battle cries.

Colin narrowed his eyes, his attention locked on a member of the cavalry who fought to stop his horse going off at a right angle to the attack.

'I think perhaps they could've done with some lessons at Moyfield,' he said, raising his voice to be heard over the villagers as they shrieked and scattered.

Marie, Kim, the girls and I had our work cut out as the re-enactment got underway. While my cavalry came under a counter-attack, I spent the next hour rounding up loose horses. They had done exactly as I had been asked. It's just that the riders had underestimated their size and power, and got somewhat carried away on hearing the call to charge. Nobody was hurt, thank goodness, and most of the riders who hit the dirt quickly climbed back on with a renewed respect, but I have never witnessed a more chaotic sight than the opening moments of that first battle. Nor had I enjoyed myself quite so much in a long time, I realised, as we began the process of transporting the horses home. So, when the call came through from the society to thank me, and ask if I would continue to supply horses as a going concern, I jumped at the chance.

Over the years, throughout the 1970s and into the new millenium, I travelled across the country to assist in battle re-enactments, from Winchcombe Hill to Blackburn, Nantwich and Sherborne Castle. I may not have heard of the association when they first approached me, but the Sealed Knot grew steadily in both numbers and popularity, earning widespread recognition for their efforts, and it continues to thrive to this day. As a result of my association with the club, some of my horses even ventured onto the silver screen. When the makers of 'The Scarlet Pimpernel' approached me, seeking mounts for cast members that included Anthony Andrews, naturally I jumped at the opportunity. It involved shooting on location for a day, in which Anthony was to take part in a horse race. Everyone wanted to come with me, including a young man called Dougie Littlewood. I had taught him to ride as a lad and he was desperate to get into film. Dougie made the cut as well, as a flag man at the end of the race, but had to sacrifice an impressive beard and moustache for the opportunity. As for Anthony himself, he was such a charming man. After filming wrapped, he even invited me, Marie, Kim and my stable girls to drink champagne with him. Naturally, we returned to Moyfield with the girls quite smitten!

25

Flood Water

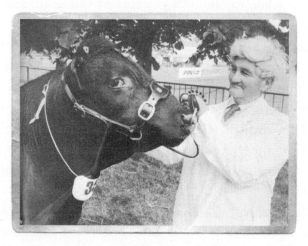

Tony at the Three Counties Show.

Horses have always been my passion in every shape or form. From teaching to riding and racing, they give me purpose and direction. But having been raised on a farm where I was always up at dawn to help my dad with milking, and gone on to marry a dairyman, cows have also been a constant presence in my life.

First there was Nimrod, who kindly permitted me to saddle her up so I could pretend she was a pony. Father's inspired decision to gift me a cow as a little girl for me to raise and sell taught me the value of livestock, and the reward that can come from patience and commitment to an animal's welfare. Tony and his father understood this better than most. As partners throughout their working lives, the pair established the oldest pedigree herd of British Friesians in Worcestershire. Together, they earned a reputation that reached far and wide.

When Trevor passed away in 1981, having seen in his seventh decade, Tony was left to manage Norval's three hundred acres on his own. It had been a slow decline for his father, and over the years Tony took on more responsibilities. Even so, he felt the loss keenly, as any son would.

Across the meadows at Moyfield, cattle seriously came back into my life when the boom years at the riding club came to an end. With a farmer's eye for spotting hardship on the horizon, I decided to invest in a Hereford stock bull. I called him JR, after the Dallas oil baron that was big on our TV screens in those days, and put him to work as breeding stock. Over the following years, that frisky young stud earned his keep all right, and helped me to establish a small herd of beef cattle. From there, I began to expand the numbers. It was a venture that served to provide me with a vital source of income, and ensured the future of my riding school.

Without a doubt, cattle have been responsible for keeping both Collins and Bomfords in business throughout several generations. They have seen us through a golden age and served us well when times became tough. Through every chapter of my life, beef and dairy cows have each played a role, and I would do everything in my power to keep it that way. They're mostly gentle, docile livestock that offer value in so many different ways, and our life with them as a family is inextricably bound. So I will never forget one fateful day when Tony and I were faced with losing a stricken herd and with it our entire livelihood.

The River Avon runs through the Vale of Evesham. It's a broad stretch of water that meanders in a crescent through miles of low-lying meadowland between Stratford-upon-Avon and Tewkesbury. At times of heavy rainfall, this pastoral watercourse is known to swell and gather strength. Through the years, householders over-looking the river at Evesham had occasionally been forced to sandbag their doors, but nothing compares to the disaster of 2007.

That summer, heading towards July, the weather had conspired to work against us. All farmers keep one eye on the skies, whether they're raising livestock or hoping for bountiful crops at harvest, and what we repeatedly saw that year was strong bursts of sunshine interspersed with storm clouds and torrential downpours. The sporadic nature of the rain, and the seasonal heat when the skies cleared, meant the ground remained semi-waterlogged. In running lessons at the riding school, it was still possible for us to ride out but such was the slip and churn under hoof that it was safer to stick to the lanes and the indoor school. As for the fields at Norval, they quickly became so punctured and pockmarked by cattle hooves that it became quite a challenge to walk out to the herd. Even so, the farm continued to provide them with adequate pasture, as did the meadowland we had recently rented nearby. There, another eighty cattle grazed on lush pasture and drank from the Avon, which formed a boundary along one side.

That morning, marked by yet another dismal forecast, Tony had driven out to the meadows to check on the herd. It was raining hard, but he returned to report that everything looked fine.

'There's one acre for every cow down there,' he reminded me. 'That's a lot of space. It might be wet but they're all grazing happily.'

With work to be done, at the dairy and the riding school, we simply got on with things. The rain, however, just kept on falling. There was no break in the clouds that day. The sun didn't once shine through to remind us of the summer we could've been enjoying. It just continued to fall relentlessly from bruised and malevolent skies. Inside the riding school, that deluge hammered on the roof with such ferocity that I had to raise my voice so the class could hear me.

By lunchtime, when Tony joined me in the kitchen bungalow to dry off and share a bite to eat, we heard on the radio that a flood warning had been issued. I just had a bad feeling as soon as the Avon was mentioned. The look on Tony's face told me the same thing was going through his mind.

'The cattle,' I said, and rose from the table with him.

We took the lorry, along with a young farm-hand called Chris who had been helping Tony on a casual basis that summer. On the road, with the wipers struggling to keep the windscreen clear, I thought perhaps we would reach the meadows to see the river in the distance running a little higher than normal. With eighty acres for them to graze in, I decided, the cattle were unlikely to have noticed. Even so, I didn't like to think of them unattended if the river was flexing its muscle.

'They like to keep their hooves dry,' Tony pointed out as we turned off the lane and onto the track that serviced fields belonging to several different farms.

'I'm sure they'll be just fine, Mrs B,' said Chris, who sat beside me on the bench seat.

'I hope so,' I said under my breath.

I'll never forget the sight that greeted us as we came into view of the meadow. That morning, Tony had left our herd grazing happily across low-lying pasture, the Avon winding slowly beyond them under a slate grey sky. Now, we found ourselves looking out across a landscape that had transformed beyond recognition. The river hadn't simply swollen but had flooded as far as I could see. There was, effectively, no sign of the river course. The water had spread and risen so high that only the top of the fencing was visible where it curved away from the service road.

And confined to this terrible sea, split onto just two pockets of higher ground, our herd lowed in a state of agitation and distress.

'We have to save them!' I cried, and grabbed the door handle.

Tony and Chris were out of the lorry before me, only to look on helplessly.

'It's too deep to reach them,' my husband said, and that was plain to see. Not only had the river burst its banks, the current had grown monstrously. Foliage and other floating debris could be seen surging between the fencing and the two islands. 'Don't even try it, Joan!'

He grabbed me by the arm, stopping me as I prepared to wade out to the fence line. 'It'll sweep you away in seconds.'

'But we have to do something!' Chris was pacing the water's edge looking both helpless and desperate. Even though we'd just arrived, it was quite clear that the flood level was still rising. 'They'll drown if we just leave them!'

We were all in shock, but the cattle remained our primary concern. They looked so helpless, and so far away at that moment. Most painful of all to witness were the calves. There were several on the island closest to us, and they looked petrified. I called out to reassure them, as did Tony, for they were all familiar with the sound of our voices. As we did so, the sound of approaching sirens cut through the hammering of rain on water. Someone must've seen us, or our stricken cattle, and called the emergency services.

By the time the fire engine arrived, along with a squad car, Tony had already raced away to summon help from a nearby farm. He returned with a tractor, and implored the brigade to help him attach a length of rope to the fencing in order to pull it down.

'You still can't go out to them, Sir,' warned the policeman. 'Your safety comes before the livestock.'

'They'll come,' Tony insisted, his focus locked on the officers as they worked to secure the rope to the fence. 'Just trust me like they trust us.'

Minutes later, with Tony behind the tractor wheel, the fencing gave way with a splintering crack. Apart from the post tied to the rope, the rest of that section caught the current and drifted away. As Tony and Chris hauled it in, I took a step forward with my hands cupped to my mouth.

'Come on then,' I called out to the herd closest to the lane, trying to sound as calm as I could. Several cows on that island flicked their ears. 'You can do it. Every single one of you!'

Tony quickly joined my appeal, his voice deeper and more urgent. A moment later, the first cow shuffled into the water as if answering the call for milking. Even from where we looked on, I could see her eyes bulge as she pushed deeper; her reluctance to go further at odds with the primal draw of familiar voices. Behind her, another cow followed suit, and then the herd instinct took over.

'That's my girl!' I cried as the cow at the front stopped wading and began to swim. 'You're nearly home and dry!'

Over the course of the next few minutes, we witnessed over forty cows follow each other into the cross-current. It was an uplifting sight at first, but also unbearable. The first cow to panic and struggle saw everyone on the service road urge her to keep fighting, but the undertow was ferocious. She wasn't the only one to be washed away, and when the calves went I couldn't watch. Worst of all, the noise they made in such a state of distress drew their mothers to the very same fate. But for those we lost, tears of joy met every cow that struggled onto dry land. Once Tony, Chris and the brigade had corralled them safely on the service road, our attention turned to those still stranded on the other island. Not only was that pocket further away from us, it had diminished in size considerably. Many of the cows out there no longer had dry land to support them, and some were beginning to jostle for position.

'It's too far,' said Tony. 'They'll never make it.'

He was right. Even if we called the stricken cattle they would be fighting against the current. I didn't want to see another cow drown, but just then it seemed inevitable that all of them would perish.

'What about the gate?' Chris clapped his hand on Tony's shoulder, drawing his attention to a point where the fencing curved out into the water some distance away. The floodwater, of course, had shown no respect for such a boundary, and had submerged the main entrance into the meadow. 'If we can open it up they'll be with the current and it won't be so far for them to swim.'

We could see the top bar of the gate. I was just a dark band in the water with the fence posts on either side like a beach groyne at high tide.

'How do we reach it?' I asked, and glanced at one of the policemen as he helped the brigade with the cattle on the road. 'They'll never allow it.'

'Joan is right.' Tony sounded broken. 'We've done all we can.'

Well, Chris heard this and seemed to weigh up the situation in his mind. Then, without warning, he broke away from us, waded out into the water and clambered onto the fence.

'Hey!' cried a voice from behind us. 'Get back here right now!'

Ignoring the command, but with all eyes upon him, that young farm-hand clambered onto the post, spread his arms wide for balance, and proceeded to cross the stock fencing as if negotiating a tightrope. I watched with my hand in front of my mouth. As he made his way out, his feet submerged deeper with every step, I really thought he would fall and drown. But he held his nerve all the way to the gate. There, clinging to the post with one hand, he fished around in the water for a moment before hauling free a loop of orange rope victoriously.

'He's done it!' cried Tony, as Chris used his foot to help the gate swing open with the current. As the rescue party sparked into action once more, I joined them in rushing to a point on the service road where I could call the cattle through. 'He's only gone and done it!'

This time, with the same level of encouragement, and with equal joy matched by horror, we saved as many cows from the flood as we could. In total, we lost eighteen cattle that day. Once the water had subsided, marked by a blessed end to the rains, we spent many grim days answering calls to drag bloated, flyblown carcasses from gullies and ditches for miles along the river course.

I still farm the meadows today, but only to grow hay for my

horses at the school. I could never risk a similar experience again, or witness such suffering from any animal. There were many heroes involved in that rescue, and when our young farm-hand, Chris, set off for new horizons he did so with my everlasting gratitude for one selfless act that saved so many precious lives.

26

The Steam Whistle

My brother John on an engine with Rex Jackson.

In her widowhood, my mother developed an inescapable fear of falling.

At first, it was just something that I noticed whenever I visited her at Quarry Pits. As a young woman with three small children and a farmhouse to run, Kitty Collins would spend her days sailing up and down the stairs without a care. In the years after Dad died, from the 1960s onwards, she'd make a point of grasping the banister firmly before taking a single step. The stairs switched around tightly from the hallway to the landing, but she never reported a slip or a tumble. Nor did she ever explain why they appeared to become steeper in her mind with every decade that ticked over. As Mother's companion at the farmhouse, Marian did her best to reassure her, but like us all we could see that she was powerless to overcome it.

In her later years, I would watch my mum negotiate each step with debilitating caution and realise how much she missed her husband. Throughout their lives together, Kitty and Colin had forged a bond that was stronger than the sum of their parts. Without him, even with our support and the solace of books, she lived a long life at the mercy of loneliness and the cruel tricks it can play.

Despite her vertigo, Kitty came alive in the company of her family and the generations that marked her lifetime. She showed as much devotion to her grandchildren as she had to Marian, John and me, while the great-grandchildren they went on to present her with were a source of delight and immense pride. Even in her final years, confined to bed and with that fear of falling closing in around her, she lit up for us all. There, especially with the younger ones, she would relive tales from a farming life that was now considered to be history. Colin Collins had been passionate about his steam traction engines. For Kitty, they came to embody her husband's spirit to the end.

Shortly before her death, having reached her hundredth year, her only son had stoked up the old Fowlers to turn the fields. In his sixties at the time, John could've used a tractor and plough, and finished the job in a fraction of the time, but he had been raised to do a job properly with tools that could be trusted. Manning one engine himself, with the firebox blazing and the boiler under pressure, Brother gave the signal to his men on the other side of the field.

'I know what they're doing out there,' said Kitty, on hearing that steam whistle, and closed her eyes contentedly as the work got underway.

Quarry Pits meant the world to John. He had moved out of the farmhouse as a younger man, only to take up residence fifty yards down the lane in a Victorian cottage. From there, he could keep a watchful eye on his livestock while staying close to his beloved engines. Our father would've been so proud of John for continuing to cultivate by steam. They shared the same sense of determination and respect for traditional agricultural methods. Neither of them were stubborn types who refused to acknowledge the benefits of advances in engineering and technology. John certainly acquired new machinery over the years, but he never gave up on the old way of doing things. Like Dad, he knew that working with steam was slow, methodical and dirty work, but he also never lost sight of the fact that when those machines were treated like living souls the results could be second to none.

Even at the seasoned age of seventy-five, John continued to work the land. Not just at Quarry Pits, but at farms across the Vale that knew they could rely on him to do a thorough job. As much as he enjoyed stoking up a head of steam on his engines, he was equally content to put his back into any kind of agricultural work. Early in August 2012, he spent one afternoon pitching several hundred bales into the barn, and the follow morning mowing forty acres of grassland just outside Inkberrow. At the time, he had three men working for him; two young lads called Gary and Andrew, and a seasoned farm-hand by the name of Albert. That same day, Brother had sent them to work on a job across the county. Dispatching Andrew on the tractor, he had ferried the others along with a trailer loaded with equipment, and then left them to it. In order to get it all home again, John had arranged to meet Andrew at Quarry Pits with the tractor that afternoon. He then planned to drive back to collect the rest of the gear and the two remaining men.

A punctual man, John arrived at Quarry Pits in good time. Once Andrew returned, he intended to take the old Land Rover out to the site, which he parked at the top of the slope in readiness. When his man didn't show up at the appointed time, John grew restless. He never liked to sit around idle. On a farm, there was always something that needed to be done. Only recently, in fact, he'd persuaded Marian to move into a little cottage he'd built especially for her, as the farmhouse was in urgent need of underpinning. John had overseen the work himself, which was almost close to completion. Rather than check on progress, however, he decided to use the opportunity to bring the cows in from the field and put them with the calves so they could feed. It was a little earlier than planned, but better than staring through the windscreen at the farm gates wondering what was keeping his man. And so, leaving his cap on the roof of the Land Rover, John set off down the slope to carry out a simple task he had completed every day for much of his life.

The field where John's cows had been grazing all day adjoined the collecting yard. By opening the gate onto the yard, he could gather the herd on this hard standing area before controlling their release into the field on the other side. There, the calves were waiting to suckle from their mothers. The cows recognised his call, of course, as my herd did with me. I have no doubt that John let himself into their field without any concerns. Even though his two-year-old bull was running with the herd, Brother was a cattleman with a lifetime of experience.

Andrew had been held up on site. When he finally made it back to Quarry Pits, he pulled up in the tractor beside John's Land Rover. With no sign of the man but for his cap on the vehicle's roof, and mindful that his boss would appreciate him catching up on lost time, Andrew made arrangements to pick up his workmates and the trailer of equipment. It was only when the trio returned that concern for Brother's whereabouts became pressing. For a man who kept such a keen eye on time, his absence seemed completely out of character.

'John?' they began to call out, on threading separate paths through the farm. '*John?*'

It was Gary who found the herd in the collecting yard. Immediately, he knew that something wasn't right. For the gate from their field was wide open, while the gate to the calves remained shut. Why John would walk away from the task halfway through was beyond him. It was as if he had encouraged them into the yard and then vanished.

Gary looked around, thinking perhaps he had been called away, which is when his attention turned to the far side of the field. At first, he believed he was looking at a sack of refuse. As a lane ran behind the hedgerow, Gary just assumed someone had been fly-tip-ping. But as he drew closer, and realised he was looking at a body, it became apparent that something far more serious had occurred.

By the time I rushed to the farm, after receiving that dreadful call, I found the police had taped off the field and forensics were out in their boots. This was no crime, however, as the coroner would conclude. Brother had suffered serious internal injuries, and though the bull was found with the cattle in the collecting yard, it didn't take much to imagine what had happened. Poor Gary suffered a terrible shock, as did Andrew and Albert. Marian was beside herself with grief. It was just an awful accident, and there was nothing anybody could've done. As my brother would have been the first to say, farming is a risky business.

It was a small comfort to know that John died at Quarry Pits. He had come into this world there, left from the very same place, and like our father before him the soil across those one hundred acres will forever contain his spirit.

John's funeral was an event that people will remember fondly for a long time to come. His coffin, built from the oak planks that he had set aside for the event in a deal with a neighbouring farmer, was carried from the farm to the church up at Dormston by the only mode of transport that befitted a man of his calling. When the Fowler ploughing engine set off with several miles of country lane to travel, the vicar had been greeting friends and family as they arrived to take their pews.

'As soon as I heard the two blasts of that steam whistle,' she would tell me, 'I knew he was on his way.'

As with my parents, who share the same headstone there, John is buried in the church graveyard. His plot sits under the branches of a mature tree, overlooking rolling fields of crops and livestock, just as it should be. Those who bore his coffin still chuckle at the struggle they faced in carrying it, built as it was from such heavy timber. In the same way, I can smile now about the moment on the way to the service when the engine's driver had to brake on a hill to stop it from running away. I did warn him about that gradient, but he had to learn the hard way, and no doubt my brother was watching over him as he successfully engaged a lower gear to complete the journey. Without doubt, John was a man for all seasons who meant so many things to so many different people, as testified by the numbers that turned out that day to bid him farewell.

As for the engine that carried my brother to his final place of rest, that old Fowler never had a name throughout its years of service. Thanks to ongoing efforts in restoration and maintenance by a local steam enthusiast, our gentle giant has found a new purpose as a working exhibit at agricultural shows and fairs. Now, as the pistons pump for the crowds that gather to watch, some might note the brass plaque upon the side that reads, simply: *John*.

John's coffin pulled by the Fowler engine he loved.

27

The One Landed Orchard

Tony and I with our granddaughter Charmaine.

In his later years, having shepherded four children into adulthood and managed cattle on pasture at Norval and Moyfield, Tony's hair turned white as snow.

Kim and Joe had been too little to remember their father with his handsome, crow-black crop. You might think that he'd look like a different man in photographs, but throughout our time together that boyish smile never left him.

Tony Bomford wasn't shy of hard work. There was always something that needed fetching, building or mending here at Moyfield or up at Norval, while the livestock took up much of his time. His father had raised him as a dairyman, and schooled him in the art of herding, milking, feed and nutrition. Everything else Tony had taught himself, and the sheds and barns that still stand today are a fitting tribute to his dedication, resourcefulness and perseverance.

As well as his working responsibilities, Tony proved to be as loyal as a husband as he was as a son. When Irene and I had our differences, he never once took sides but simply sought solutions. It was a relief to him, I think, when the atmosphere between us softened, and we had four smashing kids to thank for that. I grew to like Irene as a grandmother, and when Tony's father, Trevor passed away in the early 1980s he was at her side to support her through the loss.

My parents-in-law hadn't often struck me as being close. When I lived up at Norval, Trevor sometimes did his level best to keep out of her way. He had a passion for cricket, and whenever a Test Match was broadcast he couldn't stay away from the screen. Naturally, if Irene heard the commentary coming from the front room she took a dim view of it. Even if Trevor had worked extra hard to fulfil his daily duties around the farm, she would always take the edge off his enjoyment by floating in and placing her hand on top of the set. Then, with her focus on some imaginary point through the window, Irene's expression would tighten.

'TV's getting awfully hot,' she would say, in a way that left him with no choice but to switch it off.

Trevor didn't just give up completely. As Colin and Joe remember fondly, on visits to Norval as little boys they would often break away from cooking with their grandmother, come across their granddad glued to the screen and wonder why cricket always seemed to be played in total silence.

It wasn't until Trevor died, however, that I realised how much he had meant to Irene. For a woman who could be so self-assured, the absence of her husband seemed to strip the stitching from her. She just came undone without him. Despite the unceasing support of her son, she worried about coping and the future of the farm. Then she became spooked at being alone in such a big, isolated house, and Tony felt duty-bound to stay with her at Norval.

To begin with, it took some getting used to seeing my husband cross misty fields for his morning and evening meals with the family, and then trudge back again. But then we were both so busy that it meant the limited time we shared felt special. As my husband, he watched out for me, while the children adored having a father who could be as funny as he was wise. We would often receive phone calls from sales people hoping to place their agricultural products with us. If Tony was up at Norval when a call came through, however, whoever picked up learned to be wary.

'Would you be interested in wellington boots for your horses?' the caller would ask, often in a theatrical accent. 'Or sun cream for your cattle?'

In response to his pranks, the children discovered that their father was cursed by an inexplicable terror of spiders. Of course, the children would constantly approach him with both hands cupped together just to test his mettle, and sometimes it would be enough to send him running. Apart from changing nappies, there was nothing else that scared my husband. As soon as he walked through the door, he would embrace family life with a passion.

In a way, once he'd helped his mother to restore her confidence, Tony's return to the bungalow left us all feeling as if a lodger had come to stay. We laughed about it, of course, and Tony was often the first to crack the joke. I didn't feel so sunny some years later, however, when Irene left him with no choice but to keep her company once more. She was frail this time, and needed his assistance round the clock as much as someone to talk to. It wasn't an easy decision for either of us to make, but as a couple we had drawn strength from the arrangement the first time around, and we would do so again. If anything, a return to spare but quality time together just made us both keenly aware of the bond we had forged.

For all the demands he faced from two farmhouses, as well as his never-ending work as a dairyman and farmer, Tony often sought a little space for himself. Whenever he needed to think, away from his responsibilities, he would always take himself to the very same place. While I liked to ride out and feel the wind in my face to achieve that sense of freedom, Tony was drawn to the stillness and tranquillity of his favoured spot.

The One Landed Orchard overlooks Norval, her pastures, fields and hedgerow. It was planted with pear trees over one hundred and fifty years ago on ridge-and-furrow ground, and provided the perfect place for a busy father, son and husband to sit and contemplate the world. There, with just birdsong and breeze for company, and the occasional sight of a pheasant or hare, Tony would lose himself in thought for a while before heading back down the slope with a spring in his step. To his eyes, I suppose, it was a place of rejuvenation. It served to strengthen his commitment, to the farm as much as his family, and would forever hold a special place in our hearts as much as his.

Irene Bomford passed away in 1994. In her nineties when she left us, she had relied on the loyalty and kindness of her son to the very end. Tony took great care of her in those final years, and she recognised the sacrifice he made. By then, she had left behind the animosity she had directed at me as her son's new bride. Over forty years had passed since, at our wedding, she had looked as if the air she breathed might poison her. We had stood up to each other, on occasions, and come through it as friends as much as family. Together with Marie, Colin, Joe and Kim, I said my farewell to Irene in good time, and did so with a sense of great fondness. She was, I think, a woman who lived in a world that never quite fell into line around her, and at times that left her adrift.

Irene Bomford's decline had been slow, as it had been for her husband, which gave Tony time to prepare for the inevitable. It didn't come as a shock when the end came, and in a sense he faced the same outcome with the business. The milk industry had become a heartless master at the time, and serving it caused hardship and heartache among dairy farmers across the country. In the same way that John had taken on Quarry Pits just as the demand for steam power fell away, Tony inherited a farm on the cusp of yet another monumental change. He worked harder than ever to maintain the business, but with diminishing returns there could only be one outcome.

'The milking herd will have to go,' he told me one day, and the sadness etched across his face told me this had not been an easy decision to make.

The price at market for Tony's beloved cattle was pitiful. There was no money in dairy cows any more. Beef was the only possible realistic option, as I had learned from my own small forays into that field at the time. Having talked it through, Tony bought a few head of cattle back to Norval with the purpose of breeding them. Despite having the stuffing knocked out of him somewhat, he showed the same commitment and focus in his new venture as he would to any new task he took on. Sure enough, his perseverance paid off. Within a decade, Tony had again amassed some eighty head of beef livestock. It wasn't the same as dairy, as he freely admitted. Even though he no longer had to milk twice a day, he still missed the old life. Still, like any good farmer, my husband knew that survival required adapting to the times, and he had my support every step of the way.

Of all the challenges we faced after Irene left her son the farm, it was the red tape that proved the most testing.

Both Tony and I had grown up at a time when the fate of an agricultural enterprise rested squarely with the farmer. They could, in effect, make as much or as little as they liked with their lot in life. While many were successful, there were always one or two who fell by the wayside through mismanagement, drink, complacency or laziness.

Like his father, Tony was well aware that living off the land demanded hard graft every day of the year, and he embraced that wholeheartedly. Nevertheless, some rules that came into force during his lifetime left him at a loss for words. One such financial regulation, concerning the occupation of residential farm property, would've rendered the business unsustainable had he shuttered the house at Norval on his mother's death and continued to work the land. It presented Tony with no choice but to remain living there, as he had since the early 1980s, and continue dividing his life between work and family.

By then, however, we had grown accustomed to the arrangement, and came to rather enjoy it. Even as Marie, Colin, Joe and Kim left home in turn, and started families of their own, Tony and I carried on making the most of our limited time together. I looked forward to seeing him for meals. I'd find myself looking out across the field from the kitchen. When I saw him, my heart never failed to skip a beat. Over breakfast, lunch and supper we would always have so much to talk about, and if either of us needed advice or support we sought it from each other. Even in our sixties and seventies, having worked hard all day as neighbouring farmers, we would arrange to go out together regularly with the same spark and excitement as in our courting days.

Tony and I could chart our lives together by all the obstacles we'd had to overcome. We accepted it as farmers, and never gave up in the face of adversity or sat back when things were going well. Switching from dairy cattle to beef had helped save Norval. In the same way, taking on stock of my own had supported the riding school at Moyfield. Even so, life was a struggle. Even as we reached our eighties, it didn't get any easier from one year to the next.

In January 2014 my husband had just changed into his work clothes to feed the cattle when he suffered a catastrophic stroke. He was rushed to the Royal Worcester Hospital and admitted for a week. While my father had salvaged some semblance of his former life when struck by the same calamity, Tony was left paralysed down his left side and unable to speak. With profound difficulties in swallowing, he developed pneumonia as well as a bacterial infection, and became gravely ill. He fought valiantly, of course, just as we

knew he would, and his efforts saw him transferred to a rehabilitation unit close by. I began to make preparations for Tony's return,
and the care I would need to provide. The prospect of looking after
my husband and all the duties that farming demands seemed overwhelming. At my lowest ebb, but with my priorities clear, I decided
to downsize my cattle herd and manage as best we could. I was so
sad to see them go. When the laden transporter lorry pulled away,
leaving me standing at the end of the drive with my sons, I broke
down and wept.

'Everything will be okay,' said Colin, as Joe placed his arm around
me. 'It's just another challenge.'

'We'll find our way through it,' Joe added. 'We always do.'

Early that summer, still in the care of the rehabilitation unit, Tony
suffered another setback. He had fought so hard under debilitating
circumstances, but then his kidneys began to fail.

We knew, this time, that he was facing his final challenge in life.
With a broken heart, I made arrangements to bring my beloved
husband home to die.

Tony Bomford could only be buried in one place, and I undertook
to make that happen. His grave, up at the One Landed Orchard,
has become a place of contemplation and reflection for us all. As a
family, we take solace from the fact that from there he can keep an
eye on me. In some ways, he did just that, for on Tony's passing I
inherited his beef cattle. Having given up so many at such a bleak
time my herd is up to eighty in number now, and that supports my
riding school just fine. I'm happy about that, of course, but I'd give
up every cow, calf and horse to have my Tony back.

Joe and Colin have installed a bench in the orchard, which they
dedicated to their father. Kim and Marie often leave lovely flowers
up there, and when I visit I just like to sit as we once did to eat.
After time apart, as I learnt throughout our marriage there's always
so much to catch up on. Tony and I were always busy, but we didn't

miss a meal, did we? You and I had sixty-four very good years together, and we enjoyed each other's company throughout. We never fell out or argued. Nor did we try to change each other, which is where couples so often go wrong. You respected me as an individual, and I showed the same respect for you. Looking back, we had a wonderful life. Thanks, Tony, for everything – Love Joan xx

28

Up with the Lark

Still at it. 'There's always something.'

I am a lucky lady. Even now, in my eighties, I'm still fit and healthy enough to lead a busy life. Every day I just get up and keep going, as I always have done. Things aren't the same, of course. Losing Tony has been rough. The sense of loneliness that comes when a loved one leaves can be overwhelming, as it was for Irene and my mother, Kitty. That's why I like to keep myself occupied. More immediately, with a farm to run I can't afford to lose myself to solitude.

Over the decades, our little plot of land just big enough for a bungalow has extended to more than fifty acres. Combined with Norval's fields and pasture, that's an awful lot for a little old thing like me. Every morning, when I head out to my tractor, I remember that as a little girl I didn't think twice before climbing on board. It takes rather more effort today, but I still get the very same thrill whenever I start her up. It also makes light work of my daily tasks. With all my cattle and horses to feed, I'll pick up bales and distribute them across the fields. I love seeing all the animals amble across to greet me. They've always been good company, and make great listeners, too.

The last thing I want to do is give up on my stock. They've always been a part of my life, and I'm determined to keep it that way. Lately, in fact, I passed the test that allows me to continue driving my lorry. I have responsibilities here, and if a job needs doing I'll tackle it myself. As Tony would say, 'There's always something'.

Lately, I took the decision to stop riding. I'm just as passionate about slipping my feet into the stirrups as I am about boarding a tractor, but I worry about the consequences for my school if I fell off. Every day, people come to me for lessons, and if I couldn't teach, that would be the end of it all. In particular I love helping riders with learning disabilities take the reins. No matter what challenges they face in life, you only have to see the aura of calm and wonder that comes over them on horseback. It's a great leveller, I think, and I take a deep sense of joy and satisfaction in watching them gain so much from the experience. Even in the golden days of the holiday club, when kids would sometimes come to stay as a break from a turbulent home life, I knew that riding offered different things to all people.

My charity work has also come to mean a great deal to me. Throughout our marriage, Tony and I were always involved in the Evesham Agricultural Show. He took care of the cattle on display, and I ran the gymkhana. In the early days, the show took place on the town's Crown Meadow over several days in June. It was a fun but huge undertaking for us, and would involve transporting lorry-loads of livestock and equipment from the farm. Things got easier in some ways, and more challenging in others, when the show was unable to continue on the meadow and we offered to host it ourselves. Over one thousand spectators attended, and it transformed our rural idyll for the weekend. Tony and I didn't have a moment to ourselves, but we survived, and saw the proceeds go to the Air Ambulance.

Those days might be over now, but I still like to get involved in projects that help those less fortunate than myself. In particular, I've enjoyed raising money for those in need of mobility scooters. This was inspired by an old friend called Barry from my days growing up at Quarry Pits. When I learned that he was struggling with multiple sclerosis, I felt compelled to do something. By organising charity gymkhanas and other horse-related events, we managed to provide him with a scooter, and went on to raise funds so that eight more individuals could get out and about. I am thankful for the fact that I haven't yet felt the need to slow down, but I don't take it for granted. There are plenty of people less fortunate than me, and I want to help while I still can.

Brother John shared my values. Once, together with Marian, we inherited a small plot of land from a cousin. Between the three of us, we decided to donate it to a trust that provided homes for farming families. It was lovely to see that plot put to good use, and a surprise some years later when the trust invited us to a service at the Queen's Chapel of the Savoy. Brother and I arrived dressed up for the occasion. We were feeling very out of place but grateful for the afternoon tea that followed. Fortunately, the two guests who asked to join our table were quick to put us at our ease. 'There was no edge on them at all,' as John said afterwards when we returned to the Vale with our story about meeting Charles and Camilla.

Of course, I also have my children. They're all adults now, and I feel blessed that they live nearby. We see each other all the time, and though I'm sure they think they're looking out for me, I still keep a watchful eye on them. Marie, Colin, Joe and Kim are such delightful company, as are my seven grandchildren and six great-grandchildren. As a result, that kettle in my kitchen is rarely off the stove.

If anyone drops in they'll often find themselves tramping around the riding school or the fields to look for me. If they come by early then they won't even bother knocking on my door and just follow the sound of the tractor instead. People often say that in order to make the most of life you need to be up with the lark, and they're right. Then again, when I rise, the birds have yet to break into their dawn chorus and flit across the fields. At heart, I am the lark.

Epilogue
My Horses, My Life

With 'Rain-Kins' summer 2015.

In preparing to share this story, it's been lovely to look back on the events that have shaped my life. I'll never forget several episodes, of course, but reading through letters and diaries, as well as looking through photographs, has called back to my mind special memories that might otherwise have been lost. Some things have also come as quite a surprise. A case in point is when I realised just how many horses have graced the stables at Moyfield over the decades.

Each and every one of them has possessed a unique spirit and personality, and I want to share their names with you. Above all, having taught thousands of people across the decades, I hope that someone reading this might seek out the name of the horse they learned to ride on. If it leaves them with a happy smile on their face, even now after so many years, my job is done.

- 3 Boswells
- Abbey Dance
- Abbey National
- Abbey Rose
- Abdul
- Aidmare
- Alazan
- Alfie
- Andrex
- Antellis
- Anthony
- April Love
- Archie
- Arden Prince
- Arkle
- Arrowmint
- B-Raffles
- B-Storme
- Baby Blue
- Babycham
- Bambi
- Bambi II
- Bambino
- Banner
- Barley Bree
- Barney
- Basewell
- Bay
- Bazil
- Bear
- Bennie
- Bernie
- Bess
- Big Raffles
- Big Red
- Billy
- Billy Blink
- Bimbo
- Birdoy
- Birdy II
- Blackpony
- Blaze
- Blaze II
- Blenheim
- Bloody Mary
- Blossom
- Blue
- Blue Bird
- Blue Bonny
- Blue Clover
- Blue Magic
- Bluebell
- Bobby
- Bobby Cash
- Bozo
- Bonnie
- Bonzo
- Bow
- Boysey
- Bracton
- Brandech
- Brandy
- Brandy II
- Brandy III
- Brecon Boy
- Brecon Lad
- Bree
- Brilley

- Brillow
- Bristol Fashion
- Brody
- Bubbles
- Byzantium
- C-Simpson
- Caesar
- Candle
- Candor
- Candy
- Candy Coco
- Caprice
- Captain
- Caradoc
- Carley
- Carnival
- Carry Head
- Casey
- Cavalier Tara
- Caverall
- Celeste Lady
- Chamby
- Chamossaire
- Chane
- Charley Orb
- Charlie
- Charlie B
- Charlie Brown
- Charlie M
- Charly I
- Charly II
- Charm
- Chasta
- Cheaculy
- Cherry Brandy
- Chester
- Chestnut Honey
- Christopher Robin
- Cinderella
- Cindy
- Cleas Robinson
- Cliver
- Cloudy
- Clover
- Coco
- Coco Pops
- Colonel
- Comet
- Conan
- Connie
- Copper I
- Copper II
- Copper Stylers
- Corina
- Coud
- Countryfile – our newest foal!
- Cover Girl
- Cowboy
- Cracker
- Crackerjack
- Craddock
- Crester
- Cricklade
- Crystal
- Crystal Jubilee
- Cullis
- Cupid
- Cynara

- Cyran
- Daisy May
- Dandy
- Danny
- Daybreak
- Deakins
- Debonair
- Dee
- Desert Island
- Desert Orchid
- Desert Rhymer
- Desert Song
- Desmond
- Digby
- Digger
- Dilley
- Dimitria
- Dinah
- Dobbin
- Dobby
- Dominic
- Dongle
- Donna
- Donner
- Duffy
- Dusty
- Dusty Maiden
- Dusty Rum
- Echo
- Empress
- Escalade
- Eskimo
- Eskimo Nell
- Esuha

- Fable
- Fairlawns
- Fiddler
- Flash
- Flipper
- Foxglove
- Frazer
- Freckles
- Freddy
- Frisky
- Frosty Stardust
- Fudge
- Funny
- Gay
- Gayden
- Gentle Breeze
- George's Girl
- Ginger I
- Ginger II
- Ginger III
- Ginny
- Glen
- Gold Dust
- Gold Rush
- Gold Rush VII
- Gold Top
- Golden Blaze
- Golden Candy
- Golden Challenge (Champ)
- Golden Coronet
- Golden Crystal
- Golden Prince
- Golden Shergard
- Golden Star

- Goldie
- Goldie II
- Goldie III
- Goldie Rusty
- Goldie's Golden Boy
- Goldrush
- Goldy
- Graham
- Grasshopper
- Gremlin
- Grey Crystal
- Grey Lady
- Grossages
- Hadley
- Happy Horse
- Hard Fella
- Harry Aster
- Harvey
- Healey
- Heavenly Win
- Honey
- Honeymooner
- Hopper
- Horace
- Hot Secret
- Hugo
- Hullaballoo
- Humphrey
- Iceberg II
- Icy Silver
- Issie Rum Dust
- Italy
- Izzie
- Jack
- James
- Janey
- Jangle
- Jason
- Jasper
- Jaws
- Jayne
- Jem
- Jenny
- Jerry Junior
- Jess
- Jessica
- Jester
- Jim
- Jimmy
- Joby
- Jocker
- Joey
- John
- Jonnie
- Jubilee Lord
- Juddery
- Judy
- Jule
- Jupiter
- Just Fred
- Kate's Delight
- Kelly
- Kerry
- Kerry Gold
- Killick
- Kimber
- Kipling
- Kitty

- Kizzler
- Koski
- L–Raffles
- Lady Jane
- Ladybird
- Laramie
- Lassie
- Legal Phase
- Lightning
- Lil Sarah
- Lilleys
- Little Nixon
- Little Prince
- Little Raffles
- Little Sara
- Lollypop
- Lolonol
- Lopey
- Lord Jim
- Lord Lagton
- Lucky
- Lumpy
- Lynette
- M Penny
- M–Star
- Magic Penny
- Magpie
- Mansion Mayley
- Marble
- Marcel
- Marion May Day
- Marmalade
- Marteney
- Martini
- Marty
- Marvel
- Max
- Maxe
- Mayflower
- McIrar
- Meca
- Megan
- Melba
- Melody
- Mermaid
- Mermanda
- Merry Legs
- Mickey
- Micu
- Miller
- Miller II
- Mint
- Minty III
- Miracle
- Miranda
- Miss M
- Miss Mouse
- Miss Muffet
- Miss Muffet II
- Misty
- Misty II
- Mizzy
- Monty
- Mony
- Mookalben
- Moodeys
- Moon Spinner
- Moonlight

- Moonlight II
- Moonstone
- Morning Star
- Mr Masi
- Mr Max
- Mr Nobes
- Mr Rum Rush
- Mr Santan
- Mr Sollis
- Mr Todd
- Mookalben
- Muclue Ben
- Munity
- Murphy
- My Sweet Lord
- Mystic
- Myth
- Natalie
- Nats Abbey
- Newey
- Nicegella
- Nicerfella
- Nicky
- Nipper
- Nizafella
- Nobbin
- Noblin
- Nobling
- Noddy
- Novelty
- NuNu
- Nutmeg
- Obey
- Obi
- Oliver Twist
- Orrings
- Oscar
- Oznoe
- Paddy
- Pail
- Pancho
- Pandora
- Panhouse Silver
- Patty
- Paul
- Pavi
- Paw
- Pawed
- Paxton Flight
- Peach Melba
- Peaches & Cream
- Pearl
- Pebbles
- Peewee Prince
- Pegasus
- Penguin
- Penny
- Penny II
- Pepper
- Peppermint
- Pepsi
- Perdy
- Peter
- Peter Piper
- Phantom
- Philippa
- Pickles
- Pineapple

- Pink Gin
- Pinky
- Pip
- Pipsqueak
- Pirairy
- Pirate
- Pixie
- Planty
- Playboy
- Polly
- Polo
- Pompei
- Pony
- Poppy
- Prairie
- Prairie Gold
- Prawey
- Pride
- Pride Joy
- Prince
- Prosser
- Puff
- Puffin
- Punch
- Purdey
- Question
- Raffa
- Ralco
- Rambler
- Ranger
- Ready-Brek
- Ream Puff
- Red
- Red Rum
- Relform
- Reney
- Rhoderi
- Rickey
- Robin
- Rocket
- Rocket II
- Roger
- Roly
- Romeny
- Rosey
- Royal
- Royal Mint
- Rufus
- Rum
- Rum Punch
- Rumour
- Rupert
- Rusely
- Rusty
- Saadia
- Saffron
- Sally
- Sam
- Sand Storm
- Sandy
- Santos
- Sara
- Sara II
- Sara III
- Sarah
- Satellite
- Sava
- Scandal

- Scotts
- Selwin
- September
- September Surprise
- Shadow
- Shamby
- Shamrock
- Shamus
- Shandy
- Sharazam
- Sharion
- Sherry
- Shoe String
- Silver
- Silver Tambourine
- Simon
- Sire
- Sir Echo
- Sir Oliver
- Skippy
- Slippy
- Sllaza
- Smokey
- Smokey II
- Smokey III
- Smokey Joe
- Snappy
- Snob
- Snowball
- Sockey
- Solly
- Solo
- Sooty I
- Sooty II
- SOS
- Spangle
- Spangle II
- Sparkling Ginger
- Sparks
- Spice
- Sporting Imp
- Squeak
- Squib
- Star
- Star II
- Steptoe
- Steve
- Stewart
- Stockings
- Storie
- Storm
- Streaky
- Stumpy
- Sugar
- Sugar Foot
- Suli
- Sundance
- Sunshine
- Sweep
- Syria
- Taffy
- Taffy II
- Tally Ho
- Tanya
- Tara
- Tarquin
- Teddy
- Telmar

- Telstar
- Tempest
- Tentadore
- Teri
- Terri
- Test Sullwan
- Thunder
- Tick Tock
- Tiffany
- Tiffin
- Tim
- Timmy I
- Timmy II
- Timmy III
- Timmy IV
- Timmy V
- Tiny Dawson
- Tinzetta
- Toby Joe
- Toffee
- Tolly
- Tom
- Tommy
- Tommy II
- Tonge
- Tonya
- Toska
- Trigger
- Trigger I
- Trigger II
- Trip's Hill
- Trobley
- Trotsky
- Trotsul
- Tudor Lady
- Tudor Will
- Tulley
- Tuppence
- Tuppence II
- Tweedle Dee
- Tweedle Dum
- Twinkle
- Twinkle-Toes
- Valiant
- Vally
- Velvet
- Vixen
- Wayne
- Wee Willy Winky
- Welsh I
- Welsh II
- Welshman
- Whispa
- Wilfred
- Willow
- Willy Winkey
- Win
- Winstone
- Wood Norton
- Wood Spirit
- Zara
- Ziggy
- … and not forgetting Nimrod!

Marie, Colin Joe and Kim. 'My core'.

Acknowledgements

I have tried to fill these pages with as many characters and stories from my life as possible, but inevitably there was not room for them all. It mentions very few of my dearest friends and farming neighbours, and all the scores of staff at Moyfield through the decades that were an extended family. To the thousands of wonderful people, from young tots to senior citizens who came to be taught to ride, my world would not have been the same without them. I thank them all. I also extend my thanks to my family who are so important and the core of my life, and especially my sister, Marian, for her devotion to our mother, Kitty, and for supplying additional information. Thanks also to the BBC Countryfile team, led by Phil Kerswell, and two young ladies, Sara Cywinski and Emily Roberston for their foresight; to Rupert Lancaster and the team at Hodder & Stoughton; Matt Whyman for all his hard work in helping me tell my story, and thank you to a little fox who sent an email.